the Seduction Mystique

the Seduction Mystique

GINIE SAYLES

AVON BOOKS ◆ NEW YORK

AVON BOOKS
A division of
The Hearst Corporation
1350 Avenue of the Americas
New York, New York 10019

Copyright © 1997 by Ginie Polo Sayles
Cover photo courtesy SuperStock, Inc.
Back cover author photo by Mary Ann Sherman
Published by arrangement with the author
Library of Congress Catalog Card Number: 96-46401
ISBN: 0-380-78365-7

Library of Congress Cataloging in Publication Data:
Sayles, Ginie Polo.
  The seduction mystique / Ginie Sayles.
    p.   cm.
    1. Single women—United States. 2. Man-woman relationships—United States. 3. Mate selection—United States. 4. Sex instruction for women—United States. 5. Seduction—United States.   I. Title.
HQ800.2.S29   1997   96-46401
646.7'7'08652—dc21   CIP

First Avon Books Trade Printing: February 1997

AVON TRADEMARK REG. U.S. PAT. OFF. AND IN OTHER COUNTRIES, MARCA REGISTRADA, HECHO EN U.S.A.

Printed in the U.S.A.

OPM   10 9 8 7 6 5 4 3 2 1

To my devoted husband, Reed Sayles.
Since your favorite word is "cherish,"
let me take this opportunity to tell you
that I cherish you too!

Acknowledgments

Thank you to God, my loving husband, my dear parents, and my family for your supportiveness. Thanks very much to an adorable lady named Ernestine at the 700 Club. I can always use a prayer!

Special appreciation to Carrie Feron and Harvey Klinger. Thanks for encouragement, too, from Christine Zika and Avon Books.

Hugs & Love to handsome, well-dressed Barry Poznick; to classy, creative Earnest Winborne; to spunky, adorable Lucy Broadbent; to talented sweetheart Alexis Quinlan; to super personality Carole Monette; to generous-hearted Leil Lowndes for recommending my seminars during her own; to fun, sweet Kate Caldwell and gentleman George Ciccione; to beautiful Audrei Scott, very dear Brent Scott, Austin Scott and Grant Scott.

Contents

How to Develop a Relationship

How to Get Married

the Seduction Mystique

How to be a Man Magnet

1

Secrets of the Man Magnet

Men are wonderful!
You are wonderful!
Sex is wonderful!
—GINIE SAYLES

Television lights greeted me in bright starbursts, dissolving the audience into a fuzzy blur as I came onstage. I peered through the blazing streams of light in search of one particular woman in the audience . . . a woman I had met only one hour before the show.

And then I saw her. Debbie was seated between two men, smiling triumphantly. She sent me a thumbs-up signal and I flashed a smile back to her. Together, we had met the challenge and won.

A national television show had given me the challenge: Could I—*in just one hour*—teach a complete stranger (a woman chosen by the television show) how to use the seduction techniques I teach so that she could successfully meet men in the audience and possibly even get a date lined up *before* the show ended?

I was gambling on a stranger; yet, it was a risk I was willing to take because I know the techniques I teach work.

So, in just one hour, I worked backstage with Debbie. I taught her the three secrets of a man magnet. I taught her "magic words" for success with men. I repackaged her in "relationship clothing" and taught her "courtship body language" of how to sit, stand, and walk. Then I sent her into the audience with actual skills she could use for immediate results.

Close to the end of the live program, Debbie stood up and told the host that only an hour ago she had consulted with me and using my advice she had spoken to several men and had indeed arranged to meet one of them for dinner that evening.

You can do it, too! You can learn to meet men quickly and easily— and you can learn how to do it without ever doing anything pushy or uncomfortable. In fact, you can learn to meet men without them even knowing it was by your design.

How? By mastering the inner process of magnetism.

THE INNER PROCESS OF MAGNETISM

Inside you is a special magnet that can be activated only by you. It is a magnet that can attract wonderful men to you just about everywhere you go.

This special magnet does not require great beauty or a perfect body or even an Einstein I.Q. It is a magnet that women desperately try to create in salons, in fashions, in magazine articles, and in books . . . and yet it waits inside you.

The inner magnet is your belief system. Your beliefs about men . . . about yourself . . . and about sex can attract or repel men around you.

Your belief system can be activated by three secrets of man magnets, which are:

1. Secret magic words

2. Secret courtship body language

3. Secret flirting techniques

SECRET MAGIC WORDS

Haven't you ever wished there were magic words you could say to a man and—poof!—he would fall in love with you?

Well, there *are* magic words, but they're not what you would say to a man. There are magic words that you say to *yourself*. These words can work like a charm to change your beliefs. You must be aware that your belief system determines the way you interact with men and the way men respond to you.

There are three sets of magic words that work together to transform you, and your world with men. These magic words activate your inner magnet:

1. *Men are wonderful!*
2. *I am wonderful!*
3. *Sex is wonderful!*

When you project "Men are wonderful! I am wonderful! Sex is wonderful!" you will be a man magnet. Men will flock around you and it will not be for sex. They will be responding to your healthy delight in relationships and life!

The first set of magic words is Men are wonderful! And you must believe that they are. Sure, the jerks are out there, but you don't want them anymore. You want wonderful men. So you are going to begin saying "Men are wonderful!" These magic words help release you from unhealthy relationship patterns.

Have you ever noticed that most women follow a relationship pattern? They always get men who beat them or who leave them or who cheat on them?

Well, a woman's patterns with men can be indicated by her belief system—which is her inner magnet—about men. You set up your relationship patterns in four ways:

1. What you tell yourself about men *creates* your belief system about men.

2. What you say to others about men *reinforces* your belief system about men.

3. What you agree with about men slowly *changes* your belief system to the way others believe.

4. What you tell men about past relationships *influences* their beliefs about you and thereby how they behave toward you.

WHAT YOU SAY TO YOURSELF ABOUT MEN

If you have your radio dial set to a jazz music station, what are you going to pick up? Jazz music, of course. If you have your dial set to rap, you are going to pick up rap. If you have it set to rock, you'll pick up rock. Set your dial on the classics and you'll pick up classical music.

In the same way, wherever you have the mental dial of your belief system set determines what you are going to pick up. In order to get your body's antennae sending out and picking up the right relationship signals, you must re-set your mental dial.

And you re-set your mental dial with words. No doubt you know of voice-activated computers and voice-activated VCRs. Well, human beings have a voice-activated belief system.

You tell yourself what you want it to believe. You tell yourself enough times and you accept your words as truth. You simply say your magic words—*Men are wonderful! I am wonderful! Sex is wonderful!*—over and over.

Please note the exclamation mark at the end of each set of magic words. Just as a voice-activated VCR and a voice-activated computer cannot do your bidding unless they are energized with electricity, your voice-activated belief system cannot do your bidding unless you energize it with enthusiasm.

Say all three sets of magic words with a vibrant smile and enthusiasm to power your belief system and you have re-set your mental dial so you can tune in to wonderful men.

You may not always say what you believe, but you always end up believing what you say.

*　　*　　*

I like to borrow an analogy from career-guidance writer Barbara Sher, author of *Wishcraft*, only I like to apply it to relationships.

Pretend I am holding out a plate of cookies to you. "Want a cookie?" I ask.

You think, "It looks good, but it's probably high in fat, high in calories, made with bleached flour and loaded with sugar . . ." And even if you eat it, you may not enjoy it very much because you feel guilty about eating it.

But if a two-year-old child across the room saw me, she wouldn't even wait for an invitation. She would simply light up and exclaim "Cookie!" with delight and go for it!

And that, my dear, is exactly what I want you to do each and every time you see men. Light up and mentally exclaim "Cookie!" and go for it! This will make you an irresistible force!

Men are wonderful! The simplicity of this message cuts through all the complexities of relationships.

Psychology shows that there exists a selective process inside us that contains the following:

- *Selective vision,* which means you see what you are seeking to see.

- *Selective hearing,* which means you hear what you are seeking to hear.

- *Selective experience,* which means you experience what you are seeking to experience.

So, what is it that determines what you are seeking? The words and pictures you put into your mind to create your belief system determine what you begin seeking to see, hear, and experience.

Psychology tells us that when a woman is unable to find a man who is unwilling to commit, it is usually due to an underlying *contempt for men* that is held by the woman—and she may not be aware of it. Your magic words help counteract such contempt.

A woman's greatest key to success with men is her own belief system. It sounds marvelously simplistic and it is. The most powerful truths are often quite simple.

When I wrote the book *How to* Win *Pageants*, I interviewed several winners of Miss America, Miss Universe, Mr. Male America, and Ms. Wheelchair America contests to find out what they had in common. The power of their beliefs and the words they said to themselves to keep their belief systems tuned into winning was a compelling trait they all shared in one way or another.

One Miss America, Cheryl Prewitt, told me that when she was a little girl growing up in Choctaw County, Mississippi, her daddy owned a country grocery store, and the milkman would come several times a week to deliver fresh milk. Often he would greet her by complimenting her smile and saying that she was sure to be Miss America someday.

"Ginie," she said to me, "I *believed* him. I believed his *words*."

Years later, Cheryl heard her name called as one of the top ten finalists during the nationally televised Miss America Pageant. She stood alongside nine other women who were well qualified for the crown. Some had faces of model beauty, some had voluptuous figures.

But Cheryl said, "I wasn't worried about anyone else. I could hardly wait for the emcee to call out my name as the new Miss America. My *belief* was so strong that I *knew* I was going to win it . . ." The milkman's words had planted the seed of desire she grew up to fulfill.

In the same way, words create your belief system about men. And words will re-create your belief system and your relationships with men.

Realize that your words are powerful. Start saying "Men are wonderful!" Say it over and over until your mental dial is finally set on the right channel for meeting wonderful men.

WHAT YOU AGREE WITH ABOUT MEN

When I was teaching school, those of us who were single would meet early in the mornings in one of our classrooms to have coffee together before classes began. A lot of our conversation centered around single life—and especially about men.

It never failed that someone in our group would air a grievance about a man. One would complain her ex-husband forgot to send a child support payment. Another woman would bemoan the fact that her boyfriend dropped her to marry his secretary. Soon everyone chimed in with a relationship horror story that always depicted men as jerks.

There was one woman, whom I will call Judy, who piped up daily, complaining that she couldn't meet any men and always concluded by saying, "I don't know what I'm going to do. I can't meet anybody. I'm desperate. I'm absolutely desperate!"

One morning we were joined by a new teacher, whom I will call Sandy. Men booked dates with her up to three weeks in advance. Clearly, Sandy was a man magnet, and no one was surprised, because she was a beautiful, shapely, twenty-four-year-old. No wonder her calendar was full . . . right?

That morning, as the conversation turned sour in its usual way of ripping and shredding men, someone asked Sandy what she had been up to.

Instantly, her face lit up, and with round-eyed excitement she gushed, "Oh, Mike is taking me to the festival this weekend. He is the sweetest man . . ."

Her voice faded. All the women were silent and glaring at her in stonefaced coldness. Her open enjoyment of men had clearly alienated her from the group. She blushed uncomfortably and fell silent.

Then, a few days later, as our group met for coffee and followed its usual course, I heard Sandy say something *just to fit in.*

As Judy piped up her usual ". . . and I'm desperate," Sandy suddenly interjected, "Yes, me, too. I'm . . . desperate. I'm looking for the right man."

There was a brief pause among us. We all knew she was not telling the truth. But . . . ah . . . now she sounded like everyone else! Now, she sounded acceptable. And Sandy felt it, too. Now, she belonged.

Never again did Sandy gush happily about the merits of the men she was dating. No, indeed. She had found her niche of acceptability by saying the reverse, "I'm desperate." This became her litany among us because the more she said it, the more accepted she felt.

Then a funny thing happened. Over the course of the school year, I watched Sandy's life change in the most puzzling way. Sandy changed from being a powerful man magnet to becoming a truly desperate woman who was lonely and had a hard time getting a date—*and her physical looks had not changed.* She was still beautiful. She was still shapely. She was still twenty-four years old. And she was *desperate* for dates.

What had changed in her life? Her *words.* Only her words. Sandy had talked herself out of her success with men. Her words planted the seed that grew to take over her life.

Just to be polite, just to be one of the girls, just to be accepted, Sandy agreed with the negative words that changed the mental dial of her belief system.

To keep your mental dial set on wonderful men, you are going to have to watch what you agree with. You must keep other people's static off your mental dial or you will end up tuned in to their belief systems about men. Then you will begin attracting the types of men they attract.

That means you cannot simply agree with what your girl friends are saying about men—just to be polite. Do you want their love lives?

You are going to have to say, "No, I don't agree. I think men are wonderful." And you can't just sit silent about this. Your belief system must be immediately reinforced with a *choice* in words.

Men are wonderful! In fact, there are more wonderful men than there are any other kind. They just don't get the press. Until now. I intend to give men the good press they deserve. Don't fill up your mind with information about problematic men—or that is exactly what you will get! Forget about them and concentrate on the wonderful men who are the majority.

WHAT YOU TELL MEN ABOUT PAST RELATIONSHIPS

Never, ever tell a man how badly another man may have treated you in a previous relationship.

So often, hurtful relationship patterns are created by a woman's telling a new man how the previous man mistreated her. In turn, the new man treats her the same way. **Very few men will treat you better than the last relationship you describe**. They may seem to in the beginning, but the story is in the back of their minds, and they gravitate to it as if it were a road map to an unfamiliar highway.

When you are single there are always two questions you will be asked by a new man. The first question is, "Have you ever been married or in love or lived with someone?" If you are an adult, you will say yes to one of them, if not to all of them. The next question is going to be, "What happened?"

If you open your ruby-red lips and say, ''I caught him in bed with my best friend . . . and he slept with every woman in the city . . . and he ran up my credit cards . . . and we got evicted and he went to jail . . . and he beat the kids and he killed the dog,'' my dear, you do not need an enemy. Your own words did you more harm than an enemy ever could.

You have just told this new man how little respect another man had for you. You have also told him how little you respected yourself for putting up with it—even if you conclude your tale of horror with, ''I'll never let it happen again.''

Relationships are not that easy. Everyone is good in the beginning. It is only after we are hooked into each other that our demons come out. But if you don't let this new man know the demons that got you in your last relationship, those demons won't interrupt this new relationship.

Mark fell in love with Julie, which is why I was surprised to see him not treating her well. Finally, I asked him why he was so bad to her. He frowned and said, ''I never thought I would be, but, you know, Ginie, it bothered me that Julie loved her ex-husband enough to put up with all he did to her. The only way I can know she loves me more than she loved him is if she puts up with more from me than she did from him.''

A man may feel competitive with your past relationships. If that's the case, give him something to *live up to*, not down to.

In recent years women have been told to be open with men. Far too many women have succumbed to a moment of intimacy and laid bare the facts of previous relationship problems, only to regret it later when they have their pasts thrown in their faces in criticism or ridicule.

Often this mistreatment comes from men they are too emotionally attached with to walk out on very easily. If a man knows you have taken it once, he thinks you will probably take it again.

A man must earn the right to your honesty. He doesn't deserve it automatically. He must earn it. You don't open your front door just because someone knocks, do you? No. You ask who it is and verify that that person has the right to come into your place before you let him in. Do that much with your past.

What if I told you that I had two identical cars for sale and offered you the chance to buy one of them? I tell you they are identical cars—

same year, same make, same model, same color—and they are both pre-owned.

Then I tell you that the owner of the first car carried a zoo of animals in the backseat, which is now ripped up and smells awful. The owner blasted the radio so loudly that the speakers rattle when the radio is off. Further, he never took the car for maintenance, according to the manual, so I am not sure what kind of condition the car is in.

Then I remind you that the second car is an identical car—same year, same make, same model, same features, same color—and it is pre-owned, too.

But the owner of the second car loved the car! He had it hand-polished three times a week and vacuumed every day. Not only would he not carry animals in his car, he wouldn't let anyone smoke in his car—it smells brand-new. He played the radio so softly that the speaker system is like new. And he took it for maintenance exactly on time, according to the maintenance manual—this car runs on a dime!

Which car do you want?

You already know, don't you? You want the car that was loved, cherished, cared for, valued, treated well.

Every time you tell a man how you were treated in a previous relationship, you put a market value on yourself that tells how you can be treated in your new relationship.

Remember: You do not owe anyone your social résumé. Anytime you are harping on all the bad stuff in your previous relationships you are telling selective truth, anyway. It is just that you are telling the irrelevant, selective, negative truth that creates a pattern between you and your new man.

Reverse that process! Don't track the mud of your previous relationships onto the clean fresh carpet of your new one and expect it to remain unstained. The mud isn't relevant. The joy you bring into a new relationship today is the only thing that is relevant.

A female lawyer in Dallas said to me, "Ginie, you changed my life with this advice. After you said this, I realized that every man I had dated since my divorce had ended up treating me the same way as my ex-husband. In fact, I didn't think God made any other mold of man.

"And then I realized I had told every one of them how he had treated me. So, after hearing you on this subject, I had a date with a new gentleman and I thought 'It won't hurt to try this.' He asked what happened to my marriage. I gave him a big smile and said, 'I don't think anyone really knows all the reasons a long-term relationship ends. I think it's an accumulation of little things over time that you don't pay much attention to. But, I stayed married to him for so long because *he was so good to me*.' Ginie, this new man treats me like a princess."

Like a princess. Why? Because she described that she had been treated like a princess before. She planted the seeds in his mind with her words that men are good to her.

If you want men to treat you well, let them know other men treat you well.

So how do you answer the question "What happened?" Keep it short, simple, and benign. Donald Trump did not trash Ivana. He said, "Ivana is a wonderful woman. She's the mother of my children. We simply grew apart."

A real man magnet can never abase herself by telling a man anything bad about another man in her past. She knows the belief system of a man is formed by her words.

Real man magnets do not join into a male-bashing conversation, which would let others influence their belief systems. They know the difference. They speak well of men.

Real man magnets may not be beautiful or fashionable or have perfect figures; but the one thing they all have in common is the deep inner belief that *men are wonderful!*

2

Men Are Wonderful, Not Perfect

You may have disappointments and unresolved anger from past relationships with men. You may have fears about them. That's okay. We have all felt that way at some point in our lives.

So, if you have nothing to draw from to spark a feeling of how wonderful men are, then begin with one simple view of men . . . *compassion.*

Look at a group of men talking to each other the next time you are out. Then look at each one separately. The first one you look at may be talking confidently, laughing. He may truly be enjoying himself—yet, at the same time, he is reaching for friendship in this interaction. He needs to feel *connected* to those around him . . . just as you do.

The man you are looking at wants what you want in a relationship, too. He wants a fulfilling one-on-one relationship. He wants to love and to be loved by a woman. He wants to take her in his arms and call her darling and say all the other endearments you and all women want to hear. He *wants* this!

He wants what you want, although he may be talking about business or sports with the men around him at this moment. On a much deeper level, he—and all the men there—is fraught with insecurites you don't see. The man you are looking at is sometimes unsure about his looks.

He worries about getting old, about looking old. He worries about losing his hair. He worries about his weight, his fitness, his health, and how his body compares with the bodies of other men his age.

He worries about sex. Is he average? Below average? He worries about how he compares in bed with the man standing next to him.

He worries about success, making money, pleasing women, finding love . . . or a lasting love. And, yes, he worries about his job, debts, investments, death, and taxes.

Sound familiar? Yes. He is just like you. Exactly like you. Men may have been socialized to deal with and express these feelings differently from you. But the man you are looking at . . . the very precious man you see . . . carries the same insecurities, fears, frustrations, needs, and desires you do. *Bless his little heart.*

To retrain your view of men as wonderful, channel it through compassion.

Elizabeth had a distrustful view of men. "I have never in my life looked at any man and said 'Bless his little heart,' " she said, amazed at the idea. But that is because she had never realized that a man can be seriously flawed and still wonderful.

After our consultations, she deliberately began looking at men, thinking of their insecurities, and saying to herself, "Bless his little heart." She found a new compassion for men. And she learned that compassion dissolves the artificial barriers between men and women. You can never relate intimately with a man until you share his humanity and he shares yours. Sharing humanity begins with the force of compassion.

Men are wonderful!

RIGGING YOUR OWN SLOT MACHINE

Right now, set out a mental welcome mat in your mind that welcomes virtually all men into your life everywhere you go. This is the open and receptive signal that is vital for maximum success with men.

Have the view that just about every man you meet can fit into a slot in your life somewhere. There are slots titled "Men I Speak To" and "Men I Can Ride to Work With" and "Men I Date" and "Men I Only Have Lunch With" and so on.

Try to create and fill as many different slots of relating as you can: "Men I Have Coffee With" and "Men I Have Ice Cream With" and "Men I Can Call On to Help Me When I Need It." *You want men circulating around you, throughout your daily life.* The more slots you have, the fuller and more fun and active your life will be. In this way you create a slot machine that gives you a resource of men to draw from at any time.

Now, the nice thing about having your own slot machine of men is that you can move men from slot to slot. If you find yourself liking a man, you can move him up a slot and into more of your life.

If you find yourself not liking a man as much, simply tailor your interaction with him by moving him back a slot or two until you are relating to him on a comfortable level.

For instance, you may find that a man you speak to asks you to lunch. You don't feel interested in having lunch with him, so you make an excuse every time he asks but stay friendly so that he continues to function in your life in the "Likeable Man I Speak To" slot.

Later on, if you find yourself becoming attracted to him, simply say, "My schedule has settled down a bit if your offer is still open for lunch."

He may have an excuse, and if so, don't worry about it . . . just continue operating through the "Man I Speak To" slot. He may ask you to lunch again later on, or he may not. If not, accept the relationship as it is.

If you do have lunch together a few times and you find yourself enjoying him more, you may allow him to move into the "Men I Date" slot. If you find yourself uncomfortable with him on this level, then gently distance yourself again by becoming "busy" until you are relating with him from the "Man I Speak To" slot again.

But, in each case, you are relating on some level with him.

Incidentally, you are operating with many men at the same time in this same way, so that you always have men in your life. By rigging your own slot machine this way, you find you are never without access to men—and this is a valuable power that makes you special.

Through the slot machine method of relating with men, you never "get rid of" any decent man. You may not be romantically interested in him, but why get rid of him? Distance him nicely so that you only see him casually once a month or less.

Better yet, pass him on to a girlfriend—just don't cross him totally out of your life if his only flaw is that there is no chemistry with you. Relating casually with him on some level keeps your magnetism flowing.

PRECONCEIVED IDEAS

Dare to give up your preconceived ideas about men. When you find yourself mentally evaluating whether or not a man is worth your time, reverse your perspective. Look at each man and say, "I wonder what is unique about this man."

Make that your approach to listening to him. Try to find out his uniqueness. As you do this, you will be finding ways to relate to every man you meet. *Finding ways to relate to practically every man is the most valuable quality you can have for developing magnetism that eventually attracts exactly the men you do want.*

Don't trust someone else's opinion of a man over your own. Say to yourself, "I don't care what my best friend thinks about a man. I don't care what my mother thinks about a man. And I don't care if my dog barks at him! I am going to discover the uniqueness of each man for myself!"

When you do this—when you get rid of all your preconceived ideas about men and just discover the uniqueness of each man you will discover more about yourself.

You will discover emotions you never knew you had. You will enjoy experiences you never imagined yourself having. You will see your life opening up into an adventure. You will determine your own power as a woman, your desirability, your romance, your fulfillment ... your love story. And you will discover a lot of wonderful, wonderful, wonderful men!

We live our lives through relationships, and the more relationships we open ourselves up to, the more we experience life. Experience men without forcing them to fit into a mold.

Layer your daily life with as many relationships as you can to keep your date life teeming with possibilities for love.

3

You *Are Wonderful!*

"I am wonderful!" Say it out loud.

That is the second set of magic words. You are wonderful! Believe that you are. Your very existence is a magical moment in time. And you already have everything it takes to be loved and cherished by men. You are just learning how to use it.

Why don't you always see yourself as wonderful? Because you see yourself through the mental filter that brings to the surface all the mistakes you have made, all the regrets you have, all the times when you feel you have made a fool of yourself. You see yourself through the distorted lens of your perceived shortcomings.

YOUR WONDERFUL FLAWS

You are wonderful! You are not perfect, and neither are wonderful men. That is why you are so well matched. You are both wonderful and flawed.

But let me tell you the good side of flaws. Flaws make you interesting, distinctive. Flaws add color, texture, and dimension to the way you relate to people. If you were perfect, you wouldn't have anything in common with the rest of us. But, fortunately, you are as flawed as everyone else. Great! Welcome to the human race.

And, you are trying. There are a lot of women who are just going to bump their way through life and not even try to improve their lives— but you did. You have done a lot more for yourself than you even know.

YOU ARE A WINNER

Who are the people who buy self-improvement, life-improvement, relationship-improvement books, tapes, and videos? Successful people! Successful people are self-educating people, no matter how much education they may already have. They continue to want to improve their lives.

Successful people do not always readily ascribe the label "successful" on themselves. The word *successful* sounds like a finished state, and they usually see themselves as success-in-process. That is why they continue learning.

I know a great deal about you. You are a woman who is not willing to let life pass you by without reaching for the brass rings of what you want, more than once! If you think you can look under a rock to find one scrap more of information that will make your life more effective, you are going to look under it.

You are not just a survivor in life. You are a winner. You actively seek information to learn how to gain greater control over what happens to you. Winners do exactly that.

Like other successful people, you may not be where you want to be in life, but you are a lot farther along than you think you are! Flawed and fabulous, you are wonderful.

HOW TO BE YOUR OWN BEST FRIEND

Nine times out of ten, *your relationship with a man is only as good as your relationship with yourself.* When you love yourself, others will love you too.

To build a good relationship with yourself, you must accept that you are the ultimate authority of you. Memorize this, because that is the key to how men perceive you. Become your own best friend in the following ways.

- **Choose to like anything you have, simply because it is yours.** Be loyal to yourself and your choices.

- **Be on your side always, no matter what.** If you are not on your side, who will be? Do not be on the side of your critics—although you can seem gracious in response to their viewpoint if the situation requires it. Replace criticism with a self-compliment.

- **Don't put your life on hold waiting for Mr. Right.** Mr. Right has had a number of years to come along by now. Would you keep sitting around the house waiting for a late date to show up that way? No. So, get busy temporarily enjoying Mr. Wrong and Mr. Not-So-Right as well as a few Mr. Wonderfuls. Mr. Right will show up a lot faster.

- **Be good to yourself.** I don't know why, but there seems to be a period of time in life when it feels like no one needs you. Remember, you are someone, and you need you. I heard a saying I liked, and I used to say it over and over when I was scared: "I can count on myself. I won't let me down." Sometimes I felt that I was letting myself down and I would say it faster and more furiously—even if tears stained my cheeks: "I can count on myself. I won't let me down. I can count on myself. I won't let me down."

  I had no one else to count on, and I was scared I couldn't do it; amazingly, I found that insisting on not letting myself down worked. You *can* count on yourself, no matter how weak and ineffectual you feel at times. You won't let yourself down.

- **Treat yourself better than any man can treat you.** Single women can postpone their lives by saying, "I would go to the best restaurant if I had someone to take me there" or "I would attend the concert if I were involved with someone." Much of life passes them by in the process of waiting. I believe in less patience and more action, because people who wait just get good at waiting. For those who think that waiting is faith, I must insist that action is faith. When you really believe something, you act on it. Make a date with yourself to go to the places you have been waiting to be taken to. Go with a friend or alone. If you are not good enough to be your own date, why would you be good enough to be someone else's date?

- **No more scolding yourself—ever.** If you spill milk on the floor, don't call yourself clumsy or stupid. You wouldn't say that to a guest who spilled milk. You would laugh and say, "Oh, it's nothing!" and clean it up. Do as much for yourself as you do for a guest. Treat yourself as well as you do a guest.

- **Choose words to describe yourself generously.** Never criticize yourself, joke disparagingly about yourself, or put yourself down with friends, relatives, strangers, employers, or men. *Anytime you criticize yourself, you are giving your listener permission to criticize you, too.*

- **Don't stay involved with friends or relatives who put you down.** A loving, supportive family gives you encouragement, not criticism. If you ask advice, they will put it back on you by saying, "I know you will make the right decision." A healthy family can be trusted not to tell embarrassing stories about you to a man, not to put you down in front of a man, not to talk about your exes to a man, not to joke about you or to criticize you.

  If your family does not give you encouragement, limit your exposure to them. Blood does not impart the right to use cruel words and rudeness. They may not spank you anymore, but if they say you are too fat or getting old or ask why you aren't married yet or say anything that hurts you, they are spanking you emotionally and getting away with it! You are the one who is allowing them to treat you this way by spending time around them. Your adult life is none of their business, even if they gave birth to you. You are the ultimate authority on you. Your parents, your relatives, and your friends are not.

  This one standard of refusing to be involved with relatives who put you down can have everything to do with your success with men! Move. Stay busy. Don't live with them or near them. You must take control of your own life if you intend to have your own love life. You owe more to yourself than you do to relatives who keep you down.

- **Take positive steps to build your self-esteem.** I think learning self-hypnosis with the assistance of a good hypnotherapist can be one of the smartest moves you can make for bettering your self-confidence and your self-esteem. Self-hypnosis is not a trance. It is a relaxed state that allows you to access your belief system and emotions more effectively. Positive self-reprogramming tapes can help a lot.

- **Become comfortable with you.** Build a strong, comfortable relationship with yourself. If you are shy, you are uncomfortable with yourself. Shyness means there is some part of yourself you have not fully accepted, therefore, you think others will not accept in you. When you are comfortable with yourself, you are comfortable with other people. It all boils down to your relationship with yourself.

- **Welcome you into your life.** Right now, see yourself as a little girl sitting in a chair nearby. See her clearly. What does she look like? What is she wearing? What kind of shoes does she have on?

   Looking at her, how do you feel about her? Many of my clients say they feel detached or indifferent. Some say they feel embarrassed or ashamed. Others say that looking at her makes them feel sad or angry. Many tell me they feel uncomfortable. Feelings about her range from sweetness to hostility or feeling that she was bad or wrong or at fault.

   Look at her and identify your feelings about her. Now, realize that the little girl you are looking at saved your life. She was too tiny to understand all her circumstances and she might have undergone some pretty tough criticism, but she didn't let you down . . . she kept you alive and well to today. Quite a kid, huh?

   Now call her over to stand in front of you. Tell her what she needs to hear. That she is a good child. That you appreciate all she has done for you. That she has done a good job and you are very, very proud of her. Tell her you love her and you will never leave her. Hug her into your soul.

   It helps to talk to your "little you" from time to time. Take her ice skating or to the beach or whatever she didn't get to do when you were little, so that you get more and more in touch with good emotions, nurturing your child-self in the ways no one else did. Buy her a balloon! Fulfill her forgotten needs and you will find your adult needs becoming satisfied, too.

This is a brief but important exercise. For more in-depth work in this area, study John Bradshaw's *Inner Child*. It is well worth your time.

In the meantime, I hope that this chapter has made you realize that you are the most important person in your life—and you don't know how much fun you are going to have discovering that *you are wonderful!*

4

Sex Is Wonderful!

When I was ten years old, I remember kids talking about something I knew nothing about. Naturally, I wouldn't dare let them know I didn't understand the snappy-sounding four-letter words they were using. But I couldn't ignore the situation, either.

As I helped Mother set the dinner table one evening, I innocently asked her what one of the words meant. Her dramatic reaction scared the daylights out of me! She didn't tell me what the word meant and I knew not to ask again.

What a bind! I couldn't be "uncool" and ask the kids, risking ridicule. And I couldn't ask Mother.

Determined, I visited our public library with the list of words I'd written on a scap of paper wadded in my fist.

An hour later, I had scratched out almost every word because they were not in the dictionary. All but one word—*sex*.

SEX (seks). n. 1.a. Either of two divisions of organisms that may be classified by their reproductive function. b. The sum of the structural, functional, and behavioral characteristics of living beings that subserve reproduction by two interacting parents and that distinguish males and females. 2. Sexually motivated phenomena or behavior. 3. Sexual inter-course. [Lat. sexus]

Right. Obviously, Mr. Webster didn't want his kids to know the meaning of sex, either!

Next, I went through the card catalog, slowly locating every book on sex the library had. Not one of them was checked out. It's no won-der. The small-town library had only a few tedious and technical old medical books on the subject at that time.

I was the shortest girl in my class and small for my age. My feet touched the floor only if I sat on the very edge of the tall, hard, and old-fashioned wooden library chairs at the big tables.

It was uncomfortable, but after my mother's reaction, I was afraid to check out the books. So I sat uncomfortably at the table for a long time and studied the diagrams in each book, memorizing the terms, until I knew what sex was. That is how I learned about it.

That was the technical part of sex. The experience of sex came later. What the pictures, diagrams, and medical books did not tell me is this:

YOUR SEXUAL UNIQUENESS IS WONDERFUL

You know that each snowflake is an original design. There is never another snowflake like it. Snowflakes may look alike because of the elements they have in common, but each snowflake is a design of nature that will never again be duplicated. Consequently, there is no such thing as a superior or inferior snowflake. Each is unique. Incomparable.

Likewise, no two thumbprints are ever the same. People have traits in common and may seem alike, but each individual is a design of nature that will never again be duplicated. Each is unique. Incompa-rable.

And your precious sexuality is exactly the same way. No two women express sex exactly alike. They may have elements of sexuality in common and may seem alike, but each woman's sensuality is a design of nature that will never again be duplicated. Consequently, there is no such thing as a superior or inferior sexuality. Each is unique. Incomparable.

This is important for you to understand. Through my private consultations with women, I learned that some of them have experienced men who made innuendos about their previous lovers that made them feel inadequate, lacking, or failures as lovers.

But that cannot be. It is impossible. Your uniqueness defies comparisons forever. *Your sexual nature is as individual as your thumbprint, as unique as a snowflake.* It is precious. Treasure it.

Therefore, you should not ever try to be like someone else in bed, or you are robbing your own potential, your ultimate joy. And your sexual universe could become a wasteland. You are a wonderful and unique sexual creature. No one else in the universe has your sexuality.

BECOME COMFORTABLE WITH YOUR SEXUALITY

Start where you are. If you are not yet experiencing orgasms, begin focusing on what you do enjoy about sex. Do you like the closeness? Do you enjoy his arms around you? Or the weight of his body on yours?

Identify what is enjoyable for you even if it is just the warmth of the bed when you and he are lying together afterward. Or his masculine scent, or his contentment that envelops both of you. Start with pleasurable details and build a collection of sexual desires.

Dismiss any disappointments you may feel about sex or about yourself or about having orgasms. Banish them from your bedroom and *focus* only on what you like. Focus and fully surrender yourself into these magnificent details of pleasure in your sex life.

One purpose of sex is enjoyment of each other. Promise yourself that if you never experience an orgasm in your life you will not be robbed of the garden of pleasures you are able to enjoy sexually with a man. This is far more important for your happiness and your relationships.

You stand a much greater chance of experiencing orgasms if you do this than the woman who mentally picks over her sense of failure about it. Plus, orgasms or not, through your collection of desires, you will always enjoy sex—and that is the whole point!

HOW TO HAVE WONDERFUL SEX

Respect Sex

When the subject of sex comes up in your relationship, always indicate that you like sex. Have a wholesome attitude about sex. Do not have a junior high school mentality about it; don't act as if you are discussing something not quite nice. Listen, sex is as nice as it gets between a man and a woman. And it is much healthier than apple pie!

You have to take your hat off to sex! It has kept this planet populated for centuries—what a fabulous force and power for life! Anything that is integral with life itself has to be cherished. Sex—as a force and power of life—is integral within us, each and every one of us. Its energy is part of our personalities. It magnetizes us to each other, it bonds us to each other, it releases our energy into the world with our own special imprint.

Wonderful sex requires valuing sex itself and welcoming its mysterious complexities into you. But that is easy to do once you realize that *sex is life's desire for more life.* Something as life-propelling as that is much, much more than mere instinct or simple lust. No, sex is an actual power, a force of life that cannot be dismissed with a wink and a joke. Sex is life preservation through life perpetuation. Wow!

Have a Sex Fund

The emotion of love is the most desirable element in a fulfilling sex life. Second to that is basic skill and imagination. Still and all, a small amount of money allows you to flesh out your imagination and self-expression with purchases intended just for your sex life.

Buy a pretty container to drop extra change into at the end of a day. The container does not have to be expensive, just pretty. It may be a brass container that reminds you of Aladdin's lamp, an elegant crystal jar, or a lovely antique vase.

Your sex fund enables you to spend money, without guilt, on sensual items for your home: filmy lingerie, scented soaps, bubbly bath fragrances, soft bath brushes, plush towels, and elegant candles.

Anything we value, we put money into—education, home, clothing, vacation, holidays, friendships, retirement planning, and on and on. *Sex deserves the respect of money, of investment.* You deserve lovely self-expression in pretty panties and matching bras, sweet nighties, naughty nighties, perfume, and so on.

Have an Adult Attitude Toward Sex

Don't make a big deal out of sex. Early in your relationship and all the way up to the time you have sex together, have an adult attitude toward sex and don't make a big deal out of it. *Sex is a normal, healthy activity between two adults who respect each other as people, who desire each other sexually, and who practice safe sex.*

Limit Teasing. Anticipation and teasing play effective roles in wonderful sex, but only as they lead to fulfillment. When teasing is overused, sex can never live up to the anticipation and ultimately is a letdown.

No Lectures. Moralistic lectures are too heavy a burden to put on sex in your conversation. Resolve your guilt yourself, or just abstain—but don't burden your budding relationship with it.

Set Parameters. Sex is so important that it defines all relationships. Friend, lover, parent—all roles are defined according to their sexual nature.

Men want to know how you intend to define their role with you in sexual terms, because sex is part of romance to men.

On your first or second date, when the mood is right or when he starts to kiss you good-night, touch his arm, look him in the eyes, and say, "I want to make love with you, but I want to get to know you better first."

If you convey that sex is a possibility and that you consider him sexually desirable, a man will usually back off and respect your parameters.

It is only when a man feels that the romance of sex may never happen between you that he does not want to waste his time. He wants to find out if you consider him desirable or if you have a serious hangup. That is why he pressures you—so he can get to the bottom line about your sexual future together. A man considers sex to be part of a healthy romantic relationship.

Discuss Sex Frankly

Be a woman. And be womanly about sex. That means being aware of the importance of sex, glad to be desired for sex, and 100 percent adult about safe sex.

A man will reveal quite a bit about himself if you do not act self-righteous, shocked by his answers, or volunteer your disapprovals. If you do all that, he will say only what he knows you approve of and then you will not get the truth.

If there is resistance or embarrassment on his part, say, "If you and I are not mature enough to talk openly about sex, we are certainly not mature enough to engage in sex."

Do not ask all the following questions at one time, but do ask all of them. Interject them a few at a time into several different semicasual conversations. That way, he is less likely to tell you what he thinks you want to hear.

- "How serious do you believe the AIDS issue is?" (Asked as you and he drive past a billboard about AIDS or see a TV commercial about it.)

- "Is there anyone else you are sexually involved with?" or "How long ago were you sexually involved?" (Asked when your conversation takes on a personal tone and before you have engaged in sexual relations.)

- "How do you view monogamy? Do you use condoms? If you and I become sexually involved, are you willing to use condoms? Are you willing to have a blood test with me first?" (Asked when an interest in sex is expressed by one of you.)

- "Did you ever have an affair in your previous relationship or marriage? Did your wife?" (Asked nonchalantly when he is discussing his previous relationships.)

- "Have you used intravenous drugs socially? How long ago?" (While talking about teenagers experimenting with various substances.)

- "A lot of people have minor sexually transmitted diseases. Have you ever had to deal with any of them?" (Your nonjudgmental attitude may encourage him to open up if he does have them.)

- "When was the last time you had so much to drink that you woke up in bed with a stranger?" (Asked jokingly when he orders his third scotch. Then persist with a smile: "When?")

HOW TO BE COMFORTABLE WITH YOUR SEXUALITY

Learn to Love Your Body

You may have stood in department store dressing rooms and hated the body you saw in the mirror that didn't fit the clothes you tried on. You may have carefully gotten under the sheets and made him turn out the lights so he couldn't see your body. You may have tried to hide your body in dark colors and loose clothing. . . .

Did you know that your entire body is made up of individual living entities? Your body is comprised of tiny little cells that are alive—and they respond to your emotions. They receive direct signals from your brain and chemical changes from your emotions. They actually know you don't like them!

How much would you cooperate with someone's desire for you to do something if you knew that person hated you? That is how it is with your body. If you hate your body as a living entity, it knows it and it responds with resistance to the emotion of hate.

If you love your body as a living entity, it knows that, too, and responds cooperatively to the emotion of love.

Now, all living things respond to emotion. Animals do. Plants do. Your body does. You do. *If you want to change your body, love it into change,* just as you would a child or a pet.

Appreciate all that it does for you. Thank each organ, including your sex organs and hormones, for all your pleasure centers and for your increasing fulfillment.

Align yourself harmoniously with your body over a long enough period of time and you will see your body performing better for you. You will also notice that you are developing a rapport, a comfort, a relationship with your body that is healthy and sensuous.

Use words to insist that your body is wonderful, lovable, and lovely. If you want to change it, have the attitude that you make changes out of love for your body's better function and health, not out of hate. You will have better results. This is true whether you change your body through cosmetic surgery, diet habits, or fitness. Your body will reward you.

If you are small breasted, be adorable about it, not apologetic. Occasionally, lighten up and warn your man by saying, "Look out! Tonight, I'm wearing boobs!" Tuck small pads into the outer edges of your bra cups, underneath your breasts.

You can also tape your breasts, the way movie stars and beauty queens do. Buy duct tape or postal shipping tape (which is less painful to remove). Place one strip of tape underneath the outer side of one breast and stretch the tape strip to the outer side of the other breast, squeezing the breasts together. One more strip will anchor everything and cover your nipples. This is a good technique if you have a dressy backless dress with a plunging neckline that prohibits a bra. Remove the tape gently, in a warm shower.

He will love the cleavage peeking from your neckline and think you are fun! Be open and affectionate about it and there is no shame.

Never invite ridicule, however. Certainly, never allow a man to joke about your body. Always take the position that you feel more versatile with small breasts because you have the choice of having cleavage when you want and not having to be hassled when you don't. Be lovable about it.

You Do Not Have to Be Perfect to Be Desirable. As far as men are concerned, you do not have to have a perfect body. Get that straight and save yourself feelings of inadequacy, inferiority, negative comparisons with models or other women.

Models have talented photographers who pose them in flattering ways. They have makeup artists to make them stunning. They have touch-up specialists who airbrush them into perfection.

Many of my clients are models, and I have seen just as much heartbreak in their lives as in the lives of average women whose breasts may be smaller than their hips or whose features are not perfect.

Be a real woman that a man can relate to. Men have said to me that it isn't so much the size of breasts or hips or thighs as it is the overall care a woman gives her body that matters.

See Yourself a New Way

Wouldn't it be great to look as sensuous in lingerie as a model in Victoria's Secret catalogs? You can. How? By using the real secret of Victoria's Secret catalog models—a great photographer.

Regardless of your figure or your age, you can revolutionize your self-perception by having your own "private collection" of professionally made boudoir photographs.

Professionally made photographs by a woman photographer who specializes in boudoir photography can be best. She will approach the photo shoot as clinically as a physician. She knows how to make your body—whatever your size or shape—look feminine and appealing.

It is also an effective way to see yourself in a new light of modest sensuality. Such a picture, taken by a professional boudoir photographer, assisted by her professional makeup artist, and with you in your choice of lingerie, can be lovely. Your lingerie can make you look elegant and desirable, modest and sexy, all at the same time. You do not have to reveal anything more of your body than you wish. And you will look fabulous.

The photographer and her assistant will tell you exactly how to look over your shoulder, how to sit, and so on. They will make you feel relaxed and they will make it fun and memorable for you.

You can take some props along to fill in the background, such as:

- A few real roses or other flowers
- Children's bubbles
- A large furry throw (it does not have to be real fur)
- Throw pillows
- A teddy bear
- CD player and music you think is sexy

Many women have found that having boudoir photographs professionally made broke down many of their personal barriers of sexual self-expression and sexual self-acceptance.

Seeing yourself look as sensuous as a Victoria's Secret catalog model gives you confidence in yourself as a sensual woman, as a desirable woman. Some women have even sent the pictures to their fiancés as wedding gifts.

WHEN TO BEGIN SEX

A lot of single women complain of feeling sexually used because they went to bed with a man and he did not call back, or they lived with someone for a time and the relationship ended.

What I have found is that often a woman enters into sex with a man hoping to obligate him to come back, hoping to make a relationship out of it, hoping to get married—in other words, she was having sex with him for every reason but her own desire for sex with this man.

She had an ulterior motive for having sex with him. Without consciously thinking about it that way, she was using sex as a manipulative device—and when it did not work, she got angry and felt hurt.

We have all probably done this at some time in our lives, but you should not operate sexually that way anymore, because you end up exploiting yourself.

Relationships are not the greatest risk of all, not having relationships is the greatest risk of all. Sex does not guarantee a relationship. So, from now on, do not blame sex and do not victimize yourself because you had sex with someone and the relationship did not work out. Instead, change your motive for having sex. There is only one pure reason to engage in sex, and that is because you *desire* a man sexually.

The first time you have sex with a man should be when you know you will not feel sexually exploited later. Try this mental checklist the next time you are deciding whether or not to make love with a man.

- "Do I feel obligated to this man?" (If so, do not make love with him or you will feel exploited later.)
- "Maybe if I go to bed with him, he will like me better." (Do not make love with him or you will feel exploited later.)
- "Of course, I want to see him again, and yes, I want a relationship with him or I probably would not desire him. However, even if I knew I would never see him again, I would still want to make

love with him now. (If he is sexually safe, then you will be making love for the right reason, which is because you want to!)

You can never feel exploited, because you fulfilled *your* desire of making love with him. There is no better reason than that. There is no self-exploitation of an ulterior motive that was foiled.

SEX IS IMPORTANT TO MEN

Remember that sex is important to men in their romantic relationships. If you intend to remain celibate until you marry, be prepared to see a lot of men go by the wayside. Many men simply will not marry a woman they have not experienced sexually, because they do not want a marriage that is sexually mismatched.

However, celibacy is the safest protection from AIDS. Be true to who you are, and be aware of the fact that celibacy will cause you to lose some relationships.

If you meet a man who is willing to marry you without sex first, then I suggest you target marriage during the first six months of dating him. Otherwise, you could end up relating to each other more as buddies and never be able to rekindle the flame of passion.

Wait Six Weeks

For women who do not expect to remain celibate until marriage, a good rule of thumb is to actively date a new man for six weeks before engaging in sex with him. Earlier is okay if the issue of safe sex has been resolved and if you really, really desire him. If you are together almost constantly, and the attraction is very strong, try to hold off—at least until the fifth date.

Yes, there are women who have married men they had sex with almost immediately. I believe this happens because these couples were so in tune with each other mentally, physically, and emotionally that it would have seemed unnatural not to have made love with each other.

However, if you had sex early and a relationship did not work out, do not be haunted with regret or feel that you did something wrong. There are some attractions between a man and a woman that no one can legislate. You followed your heart. Just try to follow safe sex guidelines, as well.

Avoid Promiscuity

Promiscuous women or men do not really enjoy sex itself as much as they enjoy the thrill of defying caution. A woman who really loves sex is not promiscuous.

Do not believe anyone who says she or he loves sex too much to be careful. This is not true. Whatever you love, you protect. If you love your children, you protect them. If you love your animals, you protect them. If you love your sexuality, you protect it. Promiscuity is not protection. And it is not your partner's responsibility to protect you; it is yours.

SETTING THE SCENE FOR SEDUCTION

Part of training a man to make love to you when you want him to is to change the room slightly so that he associates certain items as forerunners of lovemaking. Eventually, just seeing the forerunners will ignite his sexual interest.

The word *sensuous* means "appealing to the senses." Sex is a culmination of pleasure through the senses: sight, sound, smell, taste, touch—and the sixth sense of suggestion.

The four elements—earth, air, water, and fire—are fundamental to sensuality. Earth can be suggested with large plants in clay pots. Fire can be suggested in fireplaces or with candles. Air and water are best suggested through music based on sounds from nature. I like recordings of tropical rain forest sounds. He just might always remember you when it rains.

Make these changes to set the scene:

Keep Him Busy

Men are happier when they are not just standing or sitting around waiting for you. So give him assignments. Have him put on the music. Have him pour the drinks. Have him carry the hors d'ouevres to the coffee table. Have him light candles, and later on, have him draw the bath. Keep him involved and he will sink more into the moment with you.

When you know he is coming over, ask him to bring something. Men become more involved if they are contributing to the moment.

You can say to him, "We are not expected at the party until nine. Bring a bottle of wine and a few CDs. I'll have some hors d'ouevres ready."

Before Sex Lighting

Fire is one of the four elements. If you do not have a fireplace, cluster candles in front of a mirror for a brilliant effect.

Before Sex Foods

Keep it light: pâté, crudités, fruit, cheese, fondue, yogurt dips, whipped cream, crackers.

Take it easy with alcohol. It dulls the senses. Alcohol is a depressant and therefore can make sex less effective. When people drink too much, they get sloppy, overly sensitive, and end up arguing or going to sleep! Too much alcohol can cause impotence in a man. Not a happy ending for a rendezvous.

If you are a nondrinker, there are good nonalcoholic champagnes and wines. Ariel and St. Regis are two nonalcoholic wines that taste great.

Mild amounts of alcohol may add to your relaxation. A single martini can be a nice aphrodisiac. One drink, sipped slowly, can assist relaxation and make for more pleasurable sex. Champagne and pinot noir are romantic wines. Two glasses should be your absolute maximum for romance.

Before Sex Dress

Archaeologists now believe that fashion evolved as a sexual attractant. Clothing, of course, was used for protection from the elements. But fashion was a way a woman could compete for male attention.

Throughout history, a woman could add trinkets to her ears, neck, wrist, or ankles. She could smear paint on her face or body or drape a swath of clothing a certain way and draw the attention of males away from other females. This was the beginning of fashion to emphasize attractive parts of her body and to camouflage other parts—hence creating fashion as an attractant.

Women still do that today. Emphasize *your* best body parts. Choose your best feature and emphasize it according to the following clothing guidelines:

Shoulders. Turtleneck sweaters, strapless dresses, spaghetti-strapped dresses.

Back. Backless dresses, interesting back straps on dresses, smoothly fitting dresses or knit tops.

Hands/Arms. Fitted sleeves, interesting cuffs, beautifully cared for nails in natural or vibrant colors, interesting rings or bracelets.

Face. Solid-colored clothing.

Bosom. Sweaters, V-neck blouses and dresses (unbutton your blouse an extra button).

Hips. Dresses that fit your hips, then flare.

Thighs. Fitted pants, leotards, short-shorts, miniskirts, slim skirts.

Waistline. Big wide belts with interesting belt buckles, dresses with fitted waistlines.

Legs. Shorts and short skirts, slit skirts, colored stockings, tights, leggings, narrow tapered pants.

Ankles. Long skirts that reveal your pretty ankles, thin ankle bracelet with Gypsy-style skirt.

Feet. Interesting sandals, sexy high heels, nail polish in bright red or hot pink, frosted white polish, one toe ring in the summer.

When he is coming over to see you for a casual evening, your clothing should not look as if you are trying to impress him. I know of a woman who put on a sheer negligee and pegnoir and spun into the room to show it to her mate. He looked at her and said, "Oh, come on . . ." Clearly, he did not deserve her efforts. Still, your before sex attire should look natural and inviting, not contrived.

When you are setting a scene for seduction, avoid making yourself look too deliberate. You can wear a pink T-shirt, tucked into a pair of fitted jeans, and go barefoot. Beneath the pink T-shirt and jeans, you can be wearing a smooth satin hot pink bra with matching panties or nothing at all! Have your brushed hair loose and full. Make sure your nails and makeup look great. Do not have a sloppy jeans look.

Sure, you want to look sexy. But what is sexy? *Sexy is a happy projection that you are "tuned in" and "turned on" to your own sexuality.* That is all it is. And any woman can be sexy.

Before Sex Talk

Your man has arrived with wine and music. You are casually but seductively dressed. You assign him the task of putting on the music and pouring wine, while you set out grapes and cheese or other foods.

He settles on the sofa, smiles as you sit beside him. His mind is relaxing into the seductive ambiance of music (sound), a sip of wine and a bite of cheese (taste), the soft fragrance of you (smell), his hands running over the furry sofa throw (touch), and his eyes' delight in you and in the room (sight).

This is going well. However, as he starts to reach for his wineglass, he see a *Time* magazine or today's newspaper headlines blaring a crisis about the economy. Suddenly, his mind jumps to his investments. Would they be better in bonds or interest-bearing accounts?

Rule 1: Put all news magazines and newspapers out of sight.

Or, while waiting for you to join him, he picks up the remote control, puts on the television, and gets interested in something going on—especially a sportscast.

Rule 2: Hide the remote control. Keep the television off.

Now, let's go back to the scene again. He has poured the wine and put on the music. You have set out cheese and grapes. He settles onto the sofa, rubbing his hand absently over the sofa throw. You slip in beside him, smile, and ask, "How was your day?"

Instantly, he recalls a worrisome message from a client he was not able to reach. His co-worker was obnoxious all day. He is not sure he can swing the sale he has been working on for months. If he launches into his "day" and the problems stewing in it, you can forget sex!

Rule 3: Keep him in the *now*.

Instead, have travel magazines, gourmet food magazines, a book of poetry. You can have a book of erotica, such as *Fanny Hill*, which does not contain a single obscene word. (Nevertheless, it was banned in America for two hundred years!)

Historic bed-and-breakfast books, romantic getaway travel flyers, and cruise brochures are all romantic fantasy literature.

He sees the travel magazines. You may ask, "Where do you think the most romantic cruise would go?"

Once he states his opinion, you give your input, too. Because a conversation does not mean that you just ask questions. It means you also give answers. However, do not disagree with him at this point. Respond positively to his idea of a romantic cruise. If you like something else, though, just say, "Oh, I agree. Your idea of a romantic cruise is ideal. I have also thought a cruise to *X* would be another romantic place."

Rule 4: Keep the conversation moving toward intimacy.

Psychological Foreplay

The talk can now lead to romantic getaway tours or to historic bed and breakfasts. Chat about making love in the same four poster bed George and Martha Washington slept in two hundred years ago.

Turn sideways and lean across his lap and chest—sitting up, though—talking all the while. Give him a light kiss and a grape. Then mention that you once read a book or saw a video about life in the American Revolution era and it had the most sensuous love scene in it.

Ask which book or video had his favorite sensuous love scene— and add, "Not X-rated. That's cheating." When he names the book or video, have him describe the love scene.

From there you can talk about places you would like to make love and ask him to name places he would like to make love. Keep the conversation moving toward personal, sensuous topics. A man is de-lighted that you are able to talk about sex in a warm, subtly exciting way. You are not being crass. You are approaching it with class.

While you are talking and listening, absently trail the nails of one hand around his hairline as you look into his eyes. This plus the music, soft lights, and a few sips of wine during all the romantic talk gradually begin to have their effect. It all soaks into his psyche, appealing to his sixth sense of suggestion. However, twenty to forty minutes is plenty of time for psychological foreplay.

Then, if he has not kissed you (and I'll bet he has), you kiss him.

Before Sex Kissing

Kissing before you get intimate is meant to invite. Use your body from your waist up. Circle your arms around his neck, press your chest against his, rub his nose with your nose, then part your lips, keep your eyes barely open, and press your lips to his.

Respond to his lip movements. Add texture and interest to your kiss by slowly moving your lips into a slight pucker, then let your lips go soft. A slow pucker, then soft. Or you can keep your upper lip still while rounding your lower lip forward into a pout and back. Lightly trace the tip of your tongue along the inner edge of his upper lip. Trace just inside his lower lip with the tip of your tongue the same way. Not too slowly on this.

Take his lower lip between your teeth and suck it inside your lip, back and forth. As the kiss ends, kiss one or both of his lip corners.

You can do all or part of these movements within one kiss. Try to vary your kisses so that they are not always the same.

Kiss Variations. The first time you kiss, have one hand holding his face. The next time run your hand through his hair. During the next kiss, squeeze him very tightly. Move your upper torso. Be there.

Kiss his ear by breathing into it, slightly puckering your parted lips onto his ear. Lightly trace his ear with your tongue and whisper non-sense. If he asks what you said, tell him it was a secret.

Kiss his neck with a series of puckered-lip kisses, then trail the tip of your tongue along an artery. Circle your tongue in the hollow of his throat and kiss the skin there. Return to his lips.

Kiss his closed eyes by circling your tongue over each, topping it with a light, gently puckered kiss.

Before Sex Touch

While you and he are talking, touch him. Trace your nails lightly along his wrist at the edge of his cuff. Trail your fingertips along his hairline at the base of his neck and around his ear.

Teasing. Teasing means to offer and to pull away. You offer something desired, then pull it away. Doing this heightens the suspense and intensity of arousal. Teasing can be applied to any aspect of lovemaking. However, do not overuse this technique or the heightened intensity can turn into angry frustration that is not fair.

Teasing is important for no other reason than for a woman to assure herself adequate arousal. Teasing is the way a woman receives the foreplay she deserves. Do not succumb until *you* are sufficiently aroused.

A common example: While locked in a passionate kiss, a man's hand rests on your knee. He slowly moves his hand up your leg. You are not ready to be touched vaginally yet. You allow him to get mid-thigh, then, kissing him deeper and more passionately (so he knows you are not really rejecting him), you move his hand away.

After a while, his hand begins moving back up your leg. You let him get higher on your thigh, then you move his hand away. More ear, neck, and lip kissing; then, here comes his hand again!

This time, you let him get much closer and enjoy it. You are almost ready for the next step, but not quite! This time, you lift his hand to your breast. And the next time his hand moves toward the clitoral area, surrender to the passion you have effectively developed in both of you.

You have led him on this far. If you are just playing around with him, stop the whole process by the second time he tries to touch you. That way, it will not be as likely to result in hurt, angry frustration for either of you.

If you tease a man too long, he may be so overly aroused that he will ejaculate early during intercourse, leaving you stranded in suspended arousal. If this becomes the norm, it can create deep wounds and lasting hurt between couples.

For that reason, a woman owes it to herself to find methods of faster arousal for herself, so she can pace herself to her partner. Yes, yes, I know. Men should pace themselves to women. I honestly believe most men try to do that. However, if you are able to accelerate this process for yourself, why not do so?

HOW TO ACCELERATE YOUR OWN AROUSAL

Be in the Now

Sexual fulfillment will not just happen. You have to "be there" for it to happen. Bring sex into the now by teaching yourself how to focus on each step of the lovemaking, such as:

- Study his face.
- Mentally tell yourself each thing he is doing: "He is kissing my palm, my wrist, my elbow . . ."
- If your attention wanders, snap it back!
- Respond, to keep anchoring your pleasure.

Soon you will find you like what he is doing and your arousal will happen faster.

Use Mental Triggers

Have you ever attended a memory-enhancement class? You are taught what I call "surreal fantasies" or "mental triggers" that quickly allow you to recall something.

For instance, let's say you meet a woman named Mary Greenstreet. You are taught to imagine seeing her face elongated into a street that is green and has a white stripe painted down the center of it. You use your brain to create a surreal fantasy as a mental trigger to shortcut your recall. This is effective because your brain remembers unusual events or unusual pictures more easily than it does ordinary ones.

The next time you see her, your mind will quickly retrieve the surreal fantasy and you will say, "Mary Greenstreet, how nice to see you."

Salvador Dalí also showed us how effective surreal fantasy is to focus the mind immediately to an idea. His most famous surreal painting, of clocks and watches melting, immediately focuses your mind on the issue of time.

Your creative brain can design mental triggers for you, sexually, in surreal fantasies that shortcut arousal. Surreal fantasies are not desires. They are incongruous images you conjure up solely for the same reason Dalí or memory experts do, as shortcuts to a goal—in this case, arousal.

You would not feel guilty about this natural process of your mind for shortcutting recall, nor would not feel guilty about using this shortcut in artistic expression, so you should never feel guilty about using a sexually surreal fantasy. It is merely a mental trigger.

Use Fantasies

Come up with your own surreal fantasy. It may be that you are making love on the stage at Carnegie Hall in front of an applauding full house or that you are giving a business presentation in the nude.

You may be a happy Victorian hostess who would never dream of saying anything but yes to any request of male guests. You may imagine yourself a wanton female who brazenly declares, "I am a wicked girl and I like to be a wicked girl!"

As long as you do not fear that these fantasies signify anything more than the mental triggers they are, you will be fine. You are using them as they are intended—to shortcut your arousal.

Surreal fantasies are better kept scripted inside your own head, where you control the outcome. To try to act them out may end up in disappointment, foolishness, misunderstandings, and hurt feelings.

Use One Intercourse as Arousal for the Next Intercourse

If premature ejaculation occurs from too much teasing, then so be it, as long as you know that another intercourse is waiting in the wings that evening.

Men vary in the amount of time they need to biologically recoup and get another erection. Sometimes it may happen quickly. On the average, it takes an hour. As men age, it usually takes longer than that.

Still, if you and your man have a high degree of "hormonal attraction" between you, it is easy for sex to happen several times in one evening during the development period of your relationship.

If you and he usually make love more than once, you can still utilize teasing before your first sex act, but then, knowing he will be able to last longer during the second encounter, use the first intercourse as enhanced arousal for the second one.

What I like about these methods for accelerating your arousal is that they are evidence that you are accepting responsibility for your own sexual fulfillment.

DURING SEX

Much of the time, sex will be spontaneous. Sometimes, however, sex can be a delicious ceremony. This can be a time for each of you to get acquainted with the other's body.

Take a Bath

With music in the background, take a warm bubble bath together by candlelight. Or, if there are flowers in the house, fill the water with flower petals.

One man was impressed with a woman when, after he had sent her roses a few days before, she filled their bathwater with all the rose petals. She told him that the roses had only a few days left and she thought this was a more romantic ending for them. He always remembered bathing in rose petals with her.

Have an ice bucket with champagne (real or nonalcoholic) and two plastic (for safety) champagne glasses. Introduce a variety of comforting touches by using a soft washcloth, a firm bath brush, a rough loofah, and a soothing sudsy bar of soap. Towel each other down with thick, fluffy bath towels.

Enjoy the Bedroom

Your bed should be covered with a washable, furry throw and some throw pillows so you do not have to pull back your covers. I think it is sexier if you don't.

On your nightstand, have a vase that contains various types of feathers and some flowers. Have handy a natural bristle brush and a soft plastic bristle brush on the nightstand, along with a smooth stone and a glass of water.

You and he may experiment with sensations from using feathers, from sprinkling just a few drops of water on each other, from long strokes with a smooth stone, or from outlining each other's features with a straw. You can brush each other's bodies gently with a plastic-bristled brush, then with a soft natural-bristled brush.

Give Each Other a Massage

Tell him you will give him a massage if he will give you one exactly like it. Start with his back. Tell him what you are doing as you go along.

Rub massage oil into your hands to warm your hands and the oil.

Place your hands quietly on his back for a minute.

Gently smooth your palms from the tops of his shoulders down to the small of his back. Do it again with your fingertips or nails. Kiss the small of his back and trail the tip of your tongue in one tiny circle. Kiss.

Using your thumbs with gentle pressure, push underneath his shoulder blades, following their natural curve upward. Do this twice. Repeat with your fingertips or nails.

Trace his hairline, both sides of his neck, and down his spine. Kiss the back of his neck and nuzzle it with your nose, breathing lightly on his neck. Kiss his ear and draw his earlobe into your mouth, sucking slightly, and release it.

Now, it is your turn. All of this tickles and feels so-o-o good.

Have him do exactly the same for you. You can even tell him each step, if he has forgotten your procedure (and he probably has, because he got lost in the enjoyment of it).

Or, if he improvises, let him, as long as it feels good and lasts as long as the one you gave. Every time he changes from one method to the next, make little sounds that encourage him.

By the time he finishes, foreplay should be under way. If not, take the lead and gently move into it. The following procedure is a guideline. You may use part or all of it as you see fit. You are encouraged to expand it with your own ideas.

One stage should move into the next stage. Strive for easy transition. Some stages may move faster than others. Some may be eliminated. Go with the flow. Do not be locked in to a specific time or number of strokes before moving on. Feel the momentum of the moment.

Stage One

Ankles. He is already sitting up. You turn over, facing him. Begin lightly brushing his ankles with your fingertips. Suggest playing "do as I do" and nibble his ankles. As he follows suit, pause to enjoy the pleasure he gives. Then nibble the tips of his toes as you trickle your nails down the sole of each foot. Pause and enjoy the same. (This gets wonderful.)

Calves. Sweep your nails upward over his calves—backs, sides, fronts, inner sides—to his knees. Circle his knees with your nails and stroke the backs of his knees tenderly.

Knees. Lightly bite his knees, making a large slow circle around each kneecap with your tongue. Do the same in the hollow behind his knees. Enjoy his reciprocal knee kisses.

Thigh Tease. Repeatedly sweep your nails upward from his knees over and around his thighs. Slow your hand movement as you get close to his penis and testicles. *Do not touch them, yet.* Instead, slowly sweep your nails back down to his knees. Do this again and again, sweeping up his thighs in different patterns so his sensations are not dulled by tickling the same spot.

Move your fingers as if you are going to touch his penis, but slow down as you approach, then reverse your hand movement back down to his knees. This can drive him slightly crazy. It can drive you slightly crazy, too, as he nears your clitoris and withdraws over and over again. If he begins to touch you, let him, and enjoy it fully.

Then, stop his hand by holding it, saying, "More, later . . ." and kiss him gently as you move his arm so he can embrace you.

Stage Two

Navel/Chest. Now push him back on his elbows or back and kiss his navel. Circle it with your tongue, then reverse the direction. Kiss. At the same time, move your nailtips up from his groin area to his chest (once or three times, as you wish), while you kiss, circle, reverse circle, kiss.

Your Breasts. Arch your back and draw his lips to your navel. Or kiss him and say, "Now me" or "I love that." You may roll over on your back or side. He will especially enjoy this (and so will you) since his hands now move onto your breasts. In fact, he may suddenly be more in his element than before. And you may find that he is quite ready to enter you at this point.

But, unless you are wildly ready for him, do not yield, yet. You deserve to enjoy all the fullness of foreplay that will maximize this event for you as a woman.

Before we go further, however, I want to talk about your response to his caressing or kissing of your breasts. Do not just lie there. Make it interesting for both of you. Move your upper body from side to side at times, causing the nipple to pull from his mouth. Keep moving your upper body—slightly—so that he has to catch the nipple with his lips. It heightens the moment for both of you.

Kiss. Now, hold his face with both hands and lift it to yours for a passionate kiss. Circle your arms tightly around his neck, pressing your body hard against his. Kisses during sex should be very deep mouth kisses with tongue thrusts and aggressive tongue movement inside his mouth. Baby bites and baby kisses on his lips.

Neck/Ears. Move from kissing his lips to warm breathy kisses on his neck and ears. Move your neck or ear to his lips for reciprocal kissing. If he doesn't, whisper, "Kiss me . . . my neck . . . my ear," and thoroughly delight in it as he does.

Chin. Follow his chinline with little bites. At the same time, move your hands—or one hand—down his chest with your nails touching his skin, slowing as you near his penis. Hover just above his penis, but do not touch it, yet. Move your hands back to his face.

Hairline. Kiss and breathe around his hairline. Run your fingers from his temples through his scalp until your hands meet at the back of his head. Run your fingers from behind his ear through his scalp in the same way. Move your fingertips from the nape of his neck upward through his scalp. Then run your nails from the front center of his forehead back. Repeat this pattern. Breathe into his hair as you do this. His scalp is very sensitive—just like yours—and you will want him to do this for you.

Eyes. Kiss each eyelid and rub the tip of your tongue over it. All the while, move your hands to his buttocks and sweep your fingertips over them, coming around to his penis. Move your hands back to his face.

Nose. Trail your tongue from between his eyes down his nose and lightly bite the tip. Rub your noses together, eskimo style.

Respond. All the while, enjoy yourself. Laugh, if you wish. Giggle. Sigh. Moan. Groan. And occasionally give a bite on his shoulder to delay his sense of mounting urgency.

Kiss and lick lip corners. By this time, you have enjoyed a session of loving foreplay. If he has not placed your hands on his penis already, touch him now.

Always be very gentle with a man's testicles. You can be firmer in holding his penis. Many men complain that women do not hold the penis firmly enough.

You have made him wait long enough. While you are kissing him, reach for his penis. Teasingly play with his penis by stroking it a few minutes, holding it firmly and moving it rythmically up and down until it is very hard. Caress his testicles from time to time.

Lubrication. If you are not wet enough, you may wish to guide his mouth to your vagina for him to moisten you with his tongue. Or you can make sure his penis is well lubricated before he inserts it into you. Praise his body and, holding his penis firmly, use your tongue as if you were licking an ice cream cone to trace the underside.

Swirl your tongue over the head and back and forth across a thin cord of skin. This is the nerve center for sexual sensation in men.

If you wish, you may slide the head of his penis into your mouth, wetting it thoroughly for your own comfort when he inserts it into you.

Regardless of who is on top, take his penis into your hand and guide it to the lips of your vagina. Before you insert it, gently move it in a circle and then from side to side. That should feel really good and should be the final preparation you need for intercourse.

Practice Safe Sex

If you and your lover are practicing safe sex, you might want to consider using an over-the-counter lubricant *instead of saliva.* Keep it next to your bed. Spread it lightly on your vaginal area, rather than having either of you practice oral sex. At this point, use a condom.

Have latex condoms with you at all times. Natural condoms do not protect against the spread of AIDS.

To maximize use of condoms:

- Be sure the condom is used when it is time.
    - Have condoms close at hand.
    - Avoid getting too aroused to use a condom.
    - Avoid rushing to get one on and messing it up.
- Be sure the condom is put on correctly.
    - A condom unrolls only one way.
    - Place it gently over the penis head and push the roll down to the base.
    - Or hand it to him and have him put it on (but you check it).
- Using spermicides with a condom can cause the condom to slip off.

If you practice oral sex, cover the area with a fresh condom. You are dealing with body fluids.

A man can lose his erection if you have to stop and go look for a condom. Putting on a condom too slowly can do the same thing. To prevent this, put a condom on with one hand while gently stroking his testicles with your other hand.

Use Body Movements During Sex

Try moving your hips in slow circles clockwise, then counterclockwise. Move your hips in forward, down, and back circles.

For the best sensation, lift your hips up, then forward. Hold that lifted position—and move up and down while keeping your hips jutted forward.

COMPENSATE FOR YOUR PHYSICAL DIFFERENCES

There comes a moment of truth when you and a lover face your physical differences, sexually.

Some women have complained to me about men not coming back after they once had sex. They thought it was, perhaps, a moral or emotional issue. In fact, when I talked to men about it, I found that if they did not go back after having sex, it was because of the differences in their sexual realities, and no other reason.

Female Sexual Reality

Your sexual reality with a man is determined by:

- **Feel**—the way you feel to a man, based on the size and wetness of your vagina, as well as on the individual slant and inner texture, which differ from woman to woman.

- **Size**—the size or fit of your vagina, determined by both depth and circumference.

- **Wetness**—the amount of lubrication your vagina produces during arousal. If there is very little wetness, entry may be difficult and even painful unless aided by saliva or over-the-counter lubricants. Excessive wetness prevents friction between the penis and vagina. Things get too slick for him to feel the contact.

Male Sexual Reality

A man's sexual reality with you is determined by:

- **Feel**—whether or not you are able to feel a man's penis is determined by his size (and sometimes your wetness).

- **Size**—penis lengths in erection vary. They may be longer, but the usual sizes are comparable to the three vaginal depths:

  - Five or less inches long.
  - Seven or less inches long.
  - Ten or less inches long.

- **Thrust**—a man's sexual rhythm and pace can sometimes compensate for a difference in his size. However, his rhythm and pace may differ from that of a woman, so that she does not receive sufficient stimulation from his movements. This is why many women prefer to be on top. They can control both rhythm and pace to fit their needs.

Depth and Length Compatibility

There is no correct, better, or preferred size for either men or women; there is only correct pairing of sizes between men and women. What feels great to one male may not to another. Also, male length and female depth have nothing to do with an individual's sexual ability or sensuality.

Circumferences

Your vaginal circumference has a certain elasticity. The vagina softens with moisture during arousal to allow it to be pliable for a man's entry. Vaginal circumference seems to be unrelated to depth and may be wide or narrow. It may be slightly influenced by bearing children, especially if you are improperly cared for medically after childbirth.

Male penis circumference varies and is unrelated to length. A man may have any length penis and be either wide or narrow.

There is no best circumference for men or women. The best is whatever snugly fits you! If a man's penis is larger around than your vagina, then you will be very uncomfortable. Likewise, if your vaginal circumference is larger than that of his penis, he will not be able to feel you.

Sexual Positions That Compensate for Size Differences

If you love this man, then take a solution-oriented approach to overcoming differences in genital fit through the use of specific positions during lovemaking. This is a compassionate, nurturing, and practical use of sexual positions. If his penis is smaller than your vagina, you have the following choices:

Male-dominant positions:

- **Pillow lift.** Elevate your hips on one or two pillows. This can be a good position with an average-length penis, too.
- **Shoulder lift.** Elevate your hips by lifting your legs over his shoulders.
- **Leg cross.** Cross one leg over the other against your chest.

Female-dominant positions:

- **Chest stretch.** Sitting atop him, stretch your legs, close together, over his chest. He moves your hips with his hands.
- **Backward Rock.** Sitting atop him, with your back to him, rock to and fro.

When a man's penis is larger than your vagina:

Side-to-side. Lie down facing each other. If he is lying on his left side, you face him, lying on your right side. Put your right leg between his legs. Wrap your left leg over him. This provides a tremendously intimate contact. You are able to kiss each other and he can easily kiss your breasts and hold you during intercourse.

This position often provides orgasms to women who have not experienced them before. This position also allows for more intense orgasms. This is mainly because of the fit this position gives and also because it requires a slow, deep pace.

Up down. With him on top, keep one leg wrapped around him, one leg down.

Sidesaddle. You are on top. Sit sideways on his lap, legs closed. His legs are also closed. This limits the depth of a longer male.

Know Why You Are There

The aforementioned procedures can be a road map for your own confidence in bed and also for making sure you are receiving pleasure as well as giving it.

The last thing I ever want you to do is to become a sexual servant by trying to please a man. While you must be a courteous partner to him and have him enjoy sex, it should not be at your expense. You are in bed with a man for your pleasure.

You must represent yourself in bed. That is your responsibility. You are not responsible for his sexuality. You are responsible for your sexual fulfillment. You are courteous, considerate, and reasonably cooperative, but you can only represent you.

Totally unselfish ladies do not have orgasms. They are there for him, not themselves. You must say to yourself, "I want this for me. I want it." And then guide your behavior and his to that end. You are there for you.

SKILLS, NOT TRICKS

It is nice to have what I call "sexpertise," but, frankly, sexual gymnastic routines can leave you worn out and distracted.

It should not seem as if you are "auditioning" for a relationship, sexually. Yes, you want your mate to enjoy sex with you—but you want him to enjoy sex with *you*, not just *sex* with you.

Men do not marry just for sex. Sometimes they will not marry a woman because of sexual incompatibility, but they will not marry her *just for sex*. Sex is part of the romance of love to a man, but sex is not exclusive to love.

Self-Expression

Sex skills should be learned and practiced until they flow naturally into your self-expression of the moment. Skills heighten the intimacy and joy you feel together. But sex tricks stick out like a sore thumb. And when they are used just to impress a man, they fail. Most of all, do not forget that gimmicky sex can become impersonal. Too many "Let's try this" and "Let's try that" gimmicks detract you from each other, from the feelings you have for each other.

If you "perform" for a man, you lose your best edge for his interest. You will be in a stronger position if he is trying to please you. You should be trying to please yourself with courtesy to him—and he will be pleased.

Men have told me that they may like the fact that a woman will perform certain acts for them, but they do not like *her* more or less for it. The woman they all agreed they enjoy most in bed is the woman who completely enjoys herself! No sexual servitude mentality.

Stay Comfortable

And while we are discussing sexpertise, *never do anything you feel uncomfortable doing*. Do not sell yourself out this way. Do not let him or anyone else make you think you are wrong or persuade you to do something you strongly oppose.

Sensual responses, warmth, movement, kisses, whispers, tender touches with your fingertips over his body are your best, strongest impression. They are genuine, simple, caring, and intimate as they flow with the mood of moment-to-moment pleasure. Much more so than breaking the mood with a surprise position. And keep in mind that frequent eye contact during sex can keep you emotionally connected to each other.

CREATE YOUR OWN SEXUAL LANGUAGE

If you do not like a word that is used in sex—change it! It seems that our world has limited sex either to medical terminology or to street talk. Why, when sex is so fabulously creative? Personalize your love talk with new words that suggest affectionate play between you and your lover. This is your sexual universe. You are in control.

Your private language sparks fun and anticipation when you and your lover are with other people and one of you begins dropping words from your private language into the conversation. No one knows that you and your mate are secretly communicating with each other about sex while carrying on a completely innocent conversation with them.

AFTER SEX

How do you feel after sex? Closer? Glad to get it over? Worried about how he feels about you? Happy? Filled with regret?

The way you handle the moments immediately after sex can make the transition for you into a comfortable or closer relationship—or it can weaken the experience for you.

Anytime you feel weakened, the relationship weakens. My goal is for you to be strengthened and then for your relationship to be strengthened as a result.

If you have unrealistic expectations about his response afterward, it can cause you to feel disappointed and to think there was something lacking in you. You, then, overreact, feel less secure, and need excessive reassurance—which puts undue strain on the relationship.

If you want sex to impact your relationship positively, avoid crying about anything, cross examination, gushing about how great it was.

Instead, be happy without regrets. Take sex in stride as natural. Talk about other things.

And remember, sometimes sex can end up every way but what you expected. Laughing about the whole thing can bring much needed relaxation to the moment and set the stage of acceptance that makes sex possible later. So, don't fret, fuss, or fume—laugh it off!

After Sex Food

Have gourmet coffee already measured in your coffeemaker, along with the water. All you have to do afterward is to turn it on and let it freshly brew. The fragrance is perfect. Add a rich chocolatey dessert as a reward, or a few mints, if he does not eat desserts.

After Sex Lighting

Do not switch to high-volume lights immediately. Transition lighting is best. Switch on one soft lamp. Talk cheerfully while you put out the candles.

After Sex Hygiene

A physician told me he knew he wanted to marry a woman when she drew up a quick bath after sex. He felt that he loved her, but he said his respect for her sense of hygiene clinched it. A disposable douche is fine; if not, freshen up with a hot washcloth before dressing.

After Sex Touch

Stay away from his genitals now. Try affectionate roughhousing, tickling, kissing, hugging, sitting closely, snuggling, holding hands.

After Sex Kisses

Post-intimacy kissing expresses approval. These convey affection, warmth, reassurance, a seal of enjoyment. Do not kiss with your upper body or your tongue this time. Kiss only with your lips.

Your kisses can range from emotional, lingering lip kisses to short, happy pecks.

5

Learning to Have Orgasms

Remember when you were a little girl, learning to play a new game? Whatever the game, you felt you would never learn it and you enviously watched the other girls zip through it triumphantly, which only made you feel increasingly inept with each mistake.

Either your lack of understanding the rules or your lack of skill—or both—eventually led to your total disinterest in playing the game at all. In fact, you began avoiding any situation when the game was suggested. You said you had to go home or that you didn't feel well, and you left.

But one day you got tired of feeling left out. You got tired of feeling inadequate. You got tired of the frustration. And you did something about it.

You went off by yourself, sat down with the game pieces and any information you had about how to play it. You read it over and over. Very slowly, you played the game, alone, practicing each move again and again. You did this several times every day until, all at once, you had it! You could play the game as well as anyone.

Orgasm is no different. Your body is the equipment. I am giving you the information. Add your determination to master the skills through practice and you can learn how.

FAKING ORGASMS

While faking orgasms is understandable, you should know that it can also actually prevent orgasms. That is because faking an orgasm keeps that all-important sex organ—your brain—from its all-important function of *concentration* during sex. Faking orgasms requires you to think about what your mate is doing so that you can pace yourself to pretend at the right time. That, alone, distracts you from the very thing you need in order to experience orgasm, which is your full attention.

THE C SPOT

You do not have to hunt for one spot in your vagina for orgasms if you use the C spot, which is the spot in your mind where you concentrate. Your Concentration is your C spot.

Let's face it, if your vagina existed apart from your brain, it would not experience pleasure, I don't care how many spots it has. Your brain is the pleasure center for your vagina.

Your mind can even override the ineptitude of a lover. It is not that I want you to overlook the ineptitude of a man, but if you are already in a situation, rely on your trusty C spot to get you through it.

CONCENTRATION EXERCISE

This exercise will effectively connect your concentration to each part of your body's response. It will develop your ability to focus and experience without judging. Enjoy it. It can work.

Read this exercise, then put the book down and go through it.

- Close your eyes. Rest your hands in your lap and be very still. Now, focus your attention on the center of your mind. See a candle there. Mentally, light the candle. Watch the flame burn brighter.

- Remove the candle but leave the flame, burning perfectly, in the center of your mind. See the colors of the flame flicker as it picks up oxygen from the air and grows.

- Feel the heat from the flame fill your head with sweet warmth. Feel your face prickle from the heat of the flame. Regather the heat from your face back into the flame. Feel your face cool.

- Watch the flame slowly descend into your throat, pausing to warm and relax your neck and shoulders. Regather the heat from your neck and shoulders back into the flame. Feel your neck and shoulders cool.

- See the flame continue to move down into your chest. Feel the heat from the flame slowly spread throughout the inner lining of your breasts. Hotter and hotter. Feel it press through the points of each nipple. Continue to feel it grow. Regather the heat from your breasts back into the flame.

- Descending through your stomach, down into your hips, the flame rests on your pelvis. Watch the flame grow brighter, more beautiful, redder, hotter. Feel intense heat from the flame spread throughout your pelvis and inner thighs. Feel the heat pulsing on your vagina. Feel your body respond exactly where the heat rests. Regather the heat back into the flame. Feel your pelvis cool.

- Watch the flame move steadily back up through your stomach, your chest, your neck, back into the center of your mind.

- Replace the candle under the flame. Blow it out.

CONCENTRATION IS BETTER THAN PENETRATION

Your true sex organ for orgasms is not your clitoris, either. It is your brain. That is why literature, movies, and pictures are able to sexually stimulate someone without touching a person's body.

To experience orgasm, concentrate in one of the following ways:

- Concentrate on the sensation of intercourse.
- Concentrate on a fantasy.

- Integrate both the fantasy and the sensation into your concentration.

Your concentration—or C spot—can be used for a surreal fantasy or for sensation.

Sensation

Some women can experience an orgasm without a single fantasy entering their heads. They concentrate on the physical sensations that build and release into orgasms.

To be most effective at this method, a woman absolutely must know her body. This means that she has explored her own sensations and has learned what works for her. The woman who operates this way has likely experimented with various degrees of touch in various areas of her body. And this woman has to be able to speak up to a man and tell him what she prefers.

If you are a sensation female, then learn to be sweetly assertive and say, "I prefer being on top" or "Let's do this on our sides" or whatever instructions you want him to follow.

Do not complain or your partner will lose confidence and interest. Instead, compliment him as you guide him—say, "I especially love the way you do so and so" as you gently move his hand from one part of your body to another. And if you respond with pleasure to those things he does that you like, he will learn your body's pleasure, too.

Surreal Fantasy

Just as surreal fantasy can be used for arousal, you can also use it during sex to hasten orgasm. This can be very handy if your mate is moving at a faster pace than you.

You can have inner dialogue along with your fantasy. One of the more common examples of this is to have a forbidden fantasy and mentally say, "I am not supposed to," as often as you like. Another, which I think is cute, is a fantasy of a little train going up a hill with the inner dialogue of, "I think I can—I think I can," and seeing it go over the top.

Integrate Fantasy and Sensation

Initially, it is best either to concentrate fully on sensation or fully on fantasy until you learn to have orgasms. After that, you can experiment with integrating the two as a way to pace yourself with your mate.

TYPES OF ORGASM

There are three accepted types of orgasm:

1. Clitoral orgasm.
2. Vaginal orgasm.
3. Uteral orgasm.

Clitoral Orgasm

Your clitoris is a mysterious and wonderful little organ that is located at the point where the lips of your vulva come together above your urethra. By stimulating your clitoris by hand or with an electric massager, you are able to experience orgasms.

Clitoral orgasms are more centralized sensations. They are an excellent way to learn your body's responses as it builds to orgasm.

They also grant you sexual release. Best of all, clitoral orgasms enable you to know what an orgasm feels like.

A man can provide clitoral orgasms for you with his hands during intercourse, or he can stimulate the clitoris orally. If he is not a skilled lover in clitoral stimulation, you can guide him with your hands while kissing him. When he becomes skilled to your pace of excitement, he can stimulate your clitoris to attain virtually simultaneous orgasm.

Clitoral orgasms are equally as wonderful as vaginal orgasms. However, clitoral orgasms can be transferred to vaginal orgasms that you can experience through intercourse.

Vaginal Orgasm

Vaginal orgasms actually require less effort than clitoral orgasms, once you learn how. They differ from clitoral orgasms because the sensations are not as centralized. Vaginal orgasms contain sensations on many levels. One nice benefit of a vaginal orgasm is that it is hands-free, allowing mutual embracing during sex. And vaginal orgasms are real and separate from clitoral orgasms.

Remember when premenstrual syndrome (PMS) was considered a myth? Those of us who suffered severe mood swings, crying, and weight gain every month that disappeared after our periods started— we *knew* it was real. It was just that nobody believed us. They did not experience it, and so they accused us of having psychosomatic symptoms. Well, now the world knows that PMS is, indeed, quite real.

The same is true of vaginal orgasms. A few decades ago, someone came up with the notion that all orgasms are clitoral. If any woman protested that she enjoyed vaginal orgasms by experiencing sensations only within the vaginal wall, they would say that it was simply the penis thrust tugging flesh leading to the clitoris.

Well, once again, those of us who had experienced clitoral orgasms and vaginal orgasms knew the difference quite well. We *knew* vaginal orgasms were real and available to other women.

We knew that the epicenter of vaginal orgasms is completely different from that of clitoral orgasms. The epicenter for clitoral orgasms is frontal. The epicenter for vaginal orgasms is interior-center, within the vaginal walls entirely.

Vaginal orgasms are not superior to clitoral orgasms, but they are sometimes perferred by some individuals.

If you already experience clitoral orgasms and want to experience vaginal orgasms, you can. I devised the following method that has worked for my clients.

To transfer orgasms from clitoral to vaginal means changing your orgasm epicenter. How?

- By retraining your body's response center.
- By calling on your friend, the C spot.

Retrain Your Body's Response Center. Buy a Sunbeam Infrared electric massager (model number 1855-1). Do *not* use the infrared heat switch. You are dealing with delicate skin tissue. The reason for using this particular massager is that it has the best massage frequency for your goals.

Many massagers are so penetrating they can actually numb the nerve endings required for the best sensations. The Sunbeam stimulates and develops them. Even so, do not overuse any massager, even the Sunbeam, or it will not be as effective.

Once or twice a day for several weeks, practice with your Sunbeam. Kneel on your bed and sit down over it. Place the center of the round, metal massage head exactly over the center of your vagina.

Do not let it touch your clitoris. Your body has become used to clitoral orgasms and does not want to have to relearn something. So, you must deprive your body of any clitoral stimulation while you are making this changeover. Your body has to learn that it must go to a new location for satisfaction. Your initial goal is to develop responsiveness in muscles and nerves within your vagina.

Switch on the Sunbeam and run it for five minutes or less. Press your vagina firmly against it. Hold to the count of six. Still touching, lift just slightly so the sensation is lighter. Hold to the count of six. Press firmly again. Hold, count six. Lightly, count six.

Use Your C Spot. Concentrate on receiving sensations into your vagina throughout each exercise. Do not let the vibrator touch your clitoris.

Squeeze your vaginal muscles together as best you can while pressing firmly against the massager and hold to the count of six. Release.

Squeeze your vaginal muscles together while lightly touching the massager and hold to the count of six. Release.

Press firmly to the massager. Squeeze, release. Squeeze, release to the count of "One-two; One-two; One-two." (One-squeeze. Two-release.) Do this several times. Repeat with the light sensation of the vibrator.

Press into the vibrator. Slowly rotate your hips—avoiding clitoral contact—so that you evaluate sensations from the pressure in different rotation points. Then just enjoy the sensations a few more seconds.

Switch the vibrator off. The goal is to awaken nerve response in your vagina, so do not go longer than five minutes.

Do this every day, the same way, for several weeks, while trying to avoid stimulating your clitoris. Note sensations around your vagina; focus on sensation inside your vagina and at the opening of the lips.

Eventually, you should begin to feel muscles and nerves within your vaginal wall respond with light sensations, involuntary contractions, or muscle twitching. Then begin full-fledged concentration on the goal of orgasm while the Sunbeam is on. Utilize surreal fantasies for accelerating arousal. A certain amount of frustration is okay. Trust your hormones to put pressure on your mind to find the new location for release. This is when your C spot focuses very strongly on the sensations between the Sunbeam and your vaginal walls and leads you to orgasm.

One day, after you have been doing this for a while, you have intercourse with a man and suddenly, physical sensations inside your vaginal walls will surprise you.

Vaginal orgasm can also be developed without a machine. You can use your hand. But the Sunbeam does a far superior job of developing deeper nerve ending and muscle response.

And vaginal orgasms can also be developed without either—simply have very frequent intercourse with your mate. However, when you are single, you do not always have a consistent relationship or the quality of relationship that allows such development.

Too, there are women who were vaginally orgasmic and who, for some reason, have been celibate for quite a while. Reentering the sex world, they feel they have lost their ability to have vaginal orgasms. This method puts them quickly back into it.

It may happen quickly. It may take several weeks. It may take two or three months. The main thing is, keep at it. Success is success. What does it matter how long it took, once you have it?

Once you have learned to have vaginal orgasms, throw the machine away. You don't need it anymore! The point of the exercise is to learn how to have vaginal orgasms during intercourse with a man.

Uteral Orgasm

Uteral orgasms occur with either a clitoral orgasm or a vaginal orgasm through contractions during either type of orgasm. It relieves much of the stress of premenstrual syndrome, alleviates menstrual cramps, and can restore an easier menstrual flow. Orgasms, my friend, are *good* for you.

STYLES OF ORGASM

Joan Rivers once said she was in a supermarket when she saw a *Cosmopolitan* magazine cover that headlined "Multiple Orgasms" and she thought, "And here I have trouble just getting my toaster to pop up!"

That pretty well expresses the pressure many women feel about orgasms. First, let me assure you that it is not better to experience one kind of orgasm over the other—and *you do not have to experience orgasms at all in order to enjoy sex and to be sexy! It is a matter of personal preference.*

I may not want to cook a meal, but I still enjoy the meal! And it is nice to have a cookbook on hand, in case I want to cook. This chapter is like the cookbook. It is not necessary if you are happy with your sex life. Still, in case you decide you want to try it, the information is here.

Multiple Orgasm

Many women who experience orgasms are already experiencing multiple orgasms and do not even know it! That is because multiple orgasms have been confused with serial orgasms. Let's clear this up.

Multiple orgasms are several orgasms *within one* orgasm. These occur as waves that build and fall, surging stronger and stronger until the final one.

Serial Orgasm

This means one orgasm after another orgasm. In other words, when you have finished one orgasm, you turn your attention to having another one, perhaps a few seconds to several minutes later.

Sustained Orgasm

This feels like one solid peak, much like a singer who holds one note for several counts. It is a clean, clear moment of release. This is often followed by a flood of warmth throughout the body and a feeling of well-being.

Simultaneous Orgasm

Yes, this does exist. Do not expect to have simultaneous orgasms every time with your partner, because several factors are involved in this experience, such as stress or weariness. But do make simultaneous orgasm a goal, because it can be very gratifying for both of you. Realistically, you can expect them to happen perhaps three to six times per year. And, yes, you can have them a lot more often than that, if your mate can delay orgasm and if you stay aware of your physical and mental timing and keep with his pace for orgasm.

Above all, remember not to burden your mate with any concerns you have about not having orgasms. You are preorgasmic, not nonorgasmic.

I know five women whose relationships were destroyed because every sex act was an effort to help her become orgasmic. When efforts met with disappointment, the men felt like failures. After a while, sex was avoided. It is not worth it. Keep your orgasm goals to yourself.

Even if you are or become orgasmic, set it aside at times and just enjoy the emotional nurturing sex can give you. You can have nurturing sex (with or without orgasm), and that is far more important to your relationship.

ORGASM AND AGE

Many women experience orgasm for the first time during their thirties or forties. Your sexuality is just beginning to ripen at age thirty, whereas sex slows down a little for men in their thirties. It begins to take them thirty minutes to an hour between ejaculations.

Sex is something you can look forward to as you age. It only gets better. You become more comfortable feeling sexy in your forties and finally break free from childhood programming and inhibitions.

Your forty-year-old mate needs more time to become aroused and more direct touching of his penis and testicles to attain an erection. He can, however, endure longer during sex, giving you more time to attain orgasm. Simultaneous orgasms are easily possible with this pairing.

In your fifties, your sexuality may move into its highest level, with the possibility of explosive multiple orgasms and serial orgasms. Your fifty-something male partner will require the foreplay you required in your twenties.

After sixty, you will want to keep as regular a sex life as possible to keep vaginal walls flexible through healthy secretions. If your sex life becomes too irregular, the ability to lubricate may drop off and sex could become more uncomfortable without artificial lubricants.

Men in their sixties have a greater need to equate sex with love and require more physical attention to the genitals for an erection.

In your seventies and eighties, you and your man may enjoy from twenty minutes to forty-five minutes of foreplay for sex—which may be why they are called the golden years! Sex is normal at these ages, and women can still have orgasms.

6

Packaging Yourself for Relationships

If you ask a man what he wants in a woman he will describe traits that sound as if he's looking for a Girl Scout. If you ask a man how he wants a woman to look, he will say he wants her to look natural.

But turn him loose and he will end up with a woman who is nothing like a Girl Scout and who wears makeup like Tammy Faye Bakker!

Please understand. He was not lying before. He simply said what he thought he was supposed to want. So you have to find out by yourself what he wants. How?

Do not listen to what a man **says** he wants in a woman. Watch what a man **responds to** in women. Overall, no matter what they say, let's look at what most men respond to:

MEN RESPOND TO CLEANLINESS

Throughout my personal research with men over the years, the foremost quality men seek in a woman is *cleanliness*. This means daily soap and water, nailbrush, toothpaste, toothbrush, shampoo, laundry detergent—all for less than ten dollars, a piddling amount of time, and a few quarters for laundry. Clean is something you can afford, and it is easy. Just about every man I studied responded to cleanliness more than to facial features, size, education, or figure.

The first sign of loss of morale is loss of self-care. Lack of self-care is associated with loss of control, whether from emotional problems, disease, alcoholism, or other destructive forces.

Sometimes the only thing you do have control over is your own self-care. If you hang on to a simple ritual of self-care, you stay in control of at least that one element. Eventually, just by controlling self-care, other things in life fall into place.

MEN RESPOND TO MAKEUP

A woman does not have to have a beautiful face, but she does have to have energy in her face. Makeup adds energy to your face with color and clear definition.

Make a pact with yourself that you will never leave your house without mascara, eye shadow, and lipstick.

Eyes and lips—you can always do that much. I use mascara for both my eyelashes and my eyebrows. Brown eyeshadow looks natural. Tinted lip gloss is fine. If you have time, you can add blush.

If your skin tone is uneven, take one minute more to add foundation. Cream base in a compact is fastest, cleanest, and easiest to carry in your purse for touch-ups.

Every two years, you should have a makeup makeover. This way you will learn new techniques to compensate for the changes of aging.

Have the makeup artist teach you how to apply it yourself to look the way he or she makes you look. I strongly urge you to locate a professional makeup artist who does models for television.

Makeup gives a woman a sense of control over her physical appearance, making her feel better about herself. And men like makeup. If men did not respond better to us with it than without it, makeup would have become obsolete long ago.

Cosmetic Surgery

When a woman is thirty-eight years old, she probably does not need cosmetic surgery. Nevertheless, she should visit a respected cosmetic surgeon for an appraisal, and revisit the surgeon every two years thereafter.

The surgeon will take photos to have on hand and can detect changes during future visits. If "maintenance surgery" is expected in a few years, she can plan for it financially.

Maintenance cosmetic surgery does not change your features; it just puts everything back in place! Other types of cosmetic surgery may be to alter your nose or thighs or chin. Be sure you locate a surgeon who specializes in the area you want changed—and be sure you view the surgeon's work on a former patient.

MEN RESPOND TO HAIRSTYLES

The most important thing to remember about hairstyles is to change them! Men are more stimulated by variety in your looks than by whether or not your hair is long.

Styles

Have your hair a length that you can wear in three different styles and wear all three styles regularly. It is important to express variety in the way a man sees you. Not extreme or weird variety, just attractive change.

No matter what he says, do it. He will like his "favorite" style even better if he doesn't see it every single day.

When my husband and I were dating, we once had dinner with one of his business associates. On the way, my husband mentioned that he had known this couple for five years, then added, "But his wife has never changed her hair." Men notice. And they need the visual stimulation of change. You can appear dowdy and dull when you do not change your hairstyle.

Study hairstyle magazines or have your stylist show you at least three different ways you can wear your hair.

Hair Length

Men absolutely do respond best to hair with some length. Medium-length hair will attract just as well (and often better) than hair flowing down to your waist.

If your hair is too skimpy, you will attract some men, but not as many as you would attract if you have it either fuller, bouncier, or longer.

Men also respond positively to chin-length, mid-neck length, collarbone length, and shoulder-length. Yes, most men tell you they want long hair. But they will appreciate it more if you don't have it the very same length all the time. Even if they fuss when you change your hair, do it anyway! Change the length, even slightly, at least once a year. Twice a year is better.

Hair Color

Which should you be—brunette, redhead, or blond? Be whichever *you* feel is really you. Above all, don't change your hair color for a man.

John Lennon, the Beatles songwriter and singer, was crazy about blond hair, so his wife kept her hair bleached just to please him.

He divorced her to marry black-haired Yoko Ono, the love of his life. Yoko Ono did not bleach her hair to please him. She kept her black hair—and he loved her and her hair.

Enhancing yourself attracts love, but to change who you are defeats the whole purpose of love. Wearing your hair in ways that a majority of men respond to will enhance your overall man appeal, just stay within the realm of who you are as a person.

If you are over forty years old, use hair color to keep yourself looking not only younger but more glamorous. (Highlights or frosting have the same effect as gray hair in a woman over forty.)

True, there are some beautiful women with gray hair, but we are talking about what most men respond to. Men do not mind your getting older, but they definitely mind if you *look* older than necessary. Remember that everyone thought Barbara Bush looked so much older than George Bush because of her gray hair?

Keep in mind that ammonia-free hair color is less damaging to your hair and less likely to cause allergy problems.

MEN RESPOND TO JEWELRY

Daytime earrings in gold or silver pick up the light and bring attention to your face. Rhinestone earrings for dressy occasions will do the same. If your earrings dangle or sparkle, they give an added dimension of motion that is eyecatching.

If you have a round face, wear long earrings. If you have a long face, wear rounder or triangular-shaped earrings.

Whereas some women look better in silver-toned jewelry than they do in gold-toned jewelry, gold is a warmer tone. However, both are pretty, and whichever you look better in, wear it confidently in earrings, bracelets, necklaces, and rings.

Do not wear a ring on the third finger of your left hand, so a man will not mistake it for a wedding ring.

A string of fake pearls, pearl-drop earrings, a dressy pearl clasp for your hair when you wear it up, and rhinestone earrings can complete your jewelry wardrobe. You do not need a lot of rhinestone jewelry.

MEN RESPOND TO NAIL CARE

Several men told me they are turned off if a woman has chipped polish on her fingers or toes or doesn't keep her nails trimmed, shaped, and really clean. They feel embarrassed to be with her and think that she doesn't take good enough care of herself.

I found a method of caring for my nails that has been miraculous! I use Nailtiques nail protein and Vicon-C vitamins. Vicon-C, which I order through a pharmacist, has no generic equivalent, as other vitamins do. Surgeons prescribe it to promote healing.

I take the vitamin three times a day, and I add a coat of Nailtiques nail protein every day. On the fourth day, I remove the nail protein with nonacetone polish remover on a cotton pad. I scrub my nails with a nailbrush and dry them with a towel. I put Burielle's Night Therapy Oil on each nail and immediately—right on top of the therapy oil—I paint each nail with Nailtiques nail protein. One coat only.

If my nails need shaping, I use an emery board from side to center on each nail before applying the protein.

For the next two days, I do the same. On the fourth day, I start all over. My nails now grow long. They don't break or peel anymore.

To have pretty, sexy feet, baby them. Wear dearskin driving-shoe moccasins (from The Sharper Image, or any western store, or Ralph Lauren) with jeans or khakis. Wear these also if you have a job that does not require you to dress up.

Wear sandals in the summer. Keep your feet lathered with creams and use pumice stone to remove calluses. I like Stevens nonfragrance cream from Wal-Mart, because it only has ingredients that are good for your skin.

MEN RESPOND TO PERFUME

Fragrance is the forgotten seduction. Do not overlook the power of fragrance. However, be very careful in your selection and use of fragrance. Soap-and-water freshness is preferred to anything that overpowers. But perfume can be an added plus if it is soft, spicy, or gently floral, sensual, and subtle.

Have a "lucky" fragrance as your signature scent. Mine is Mitsouko by Guerlain. It is the perfume that more men have stopped me on the street to ask about than any other.

A woman should have two fragrances, really. One is her signature fragrance and one is a fragrance she uses only when she wants to make love.

Your second fragrance can eventually become a psychological "anchor" in a man's mind, so that just the scent of that one fragrance turns his attention to sex with you.

A true signature fragrance is one that is made for you and for no other woman. However, it is rare to find perfumers today who can do that, so find a commercial fragrance you like and make it your own.

To find your signature fragrance—which you wear all the time until, like your signature, it is identified with you—collect samples from department stores. This will save you from buying perfumes that were great at first but after a week or two were overpowering. You can also have a spring-summer signature fragrance and an autumn-winter fragrance.

Wear one sample fragrance all day long. Apply it often that day. Use a different sample the next day. See which ones get comments from people, especially men. See which ones makes you feel special.

Once you have found it, buy it in bath gel, body cream or lotion, bath powder, and cologne spray—perfume, too, if you can afford it. Layer the fragrance.

Helen Gurley Brown recommends spraying a cotton ball heavily with your fragrance and tucking it into your bra so it will "waft from your bosom." Keep soaking the same cotton ball over and over to increase its power.

Carry a purse-size container of your fragrance and touch up twice during the day and once in the evening. The most important thing to remember is that you don't want any fragrance to be cloying in either strength or sweetness.

MEN RESPOND TO COLORS

What if you went into a flower garden and all the flowers were brown or gray? You would think they were dead. Color is the beauty of life. We gasp in awe of a field of yellow wildflowers or an English garden of brilliant hues.

And would you really buy a black-and-white television today, instead of a color TV, if they were the same price? Color sells best— and this is true in relationships.

All colors are good. Yet, you will have more power in your daily life if you understand colors and how they are best used.

Authority Colors

Gray, black, navy, dark greens, deep wines, and plums are all authority colors. This is why they are perfect for business wear and serious occasions.

Camouflage

Earthtone colors such as tan, beige, ivory, khaki-greens, rust, and dull green are all camouflage colors that say "I blend in," "I don't make waves," "Please don't single me out." These are the colors to wear when you are with family or good friends. You're just one of the girls.

The Colors of Love

Relationship colors come in two types: pastel colors and bright, vibrant colors.

Love Colors — Pastels. Pastels are pale pink, pale blue, and pale yellow. These soft, yummy colors say, "I am a relationship person," "I may be a bit shy, but I am an optimistic person."

Love Colors — Bright. Bright colors such as bright red, hot pink, bright blue, and bright white are also relationship colors. Bright colors send the messages, "I like relationships!" "I exist and I'm glad!" "Here I am, no apologies."

Bright Red. Bright red can increase your pulse rate slightly every time you look at it. In fact, you can take a product that isn't selling well, repackage it in bright red, and it will likely sell better! You are selling yourself, so repackage yourself with at least one outfit in bright red from head to toe.

No prints, just one solid shade of bright red. Perhaps a red suit with red shoes or a bright red blouse and a bright red skirt with exactly matching bright red shoes, belt, and handbag. You will look like absolute dynamite.

If you feel self-conscious and uncomfortable wearing head-to-toe red, all it means is that your self-esteem may have been a tad low and that you really do need to wear this color more often so you can get used to well-deserved attention.

Red is one of the most powerful relationship colors of all. Red is a friendly color that represents Santa Claus, Christmas, Valentine's Day, love, and happiness.

Hot Pink. Hot pink is a romantic color. It is the color of roses. *When a man dreams of a woman wearing hot pink, he is in love with her.* Wear it when you want to implant in a man's psyche the image of you in roses, because you want him to love you.

White. For relationships, bright white is quite powerful. In fact, bright white from head to toe draws eyes to you just as red does. More women have won the Miss America Pageant wearing white than any other color. It is not because white seems virginal; it is because solid, bright white draws the eye to it, even from a stage.

Black. Black is a power color and therefore is an authority color. In fact, *when a man dreams of a woman wearing black, he considers her too stern, too severe.* For that reason, wear black only in the sexy sense of lingerie and in the glamorous sense of dressy fabrics such as sheer organza or black lace or black velvet or knit.

You can make black more relationship-oriented with bright gold jewelry and gold accessories on a solid black outfit. If you wear black in the evening, add glittery rhinestones or wear a gown of black sequins. One other use of solid black can work in a strapless, slinky evening gown.

Black can be aging, so use it wisely. Also, many people wear black to feel "safe." You seem less safe and more exciting if you wear color more than black. Black can be a great, sharp dressy color, but use it sparingly for impact.

Beige. Beige is not a relationship color, but if it is paired with bright white—say, khaki shorts and a crisp white shirt—it makes a casual look that is okay for relationship clothing.

Solids or Prints

Have you ever seen film clips of Queen Elizabeth in her younger days? She was typically dressed for a public appearance in one solid color from head to toe. She might be wearing hot pink. In that case, she had on a hot pink hat, a hot pink blouse, a hot pink jacket, a hot pink skirt, hot pink shoes, hot pink purse, hot pink or white gloves and a hot pink belt.

Why? Because when you look into a crowd of people, your eyes cut through the jumbled mix of color most people wear and go straight to the woman in the solid, head-to-toe hot pink—in this case, Queen Elizabeth. In recent years she has been wearing camouflage colors that will not distract from her son, who is close to ascending to the throne.

There is "visual power" in solid, head-to-toe color! Also, when you wear solid colors, your face shows up more. There are no patterns or prints competing with your face. I once read that Audrey Hepburn usually did not wear prints for that very reason.

MEN RESPOND TO SOPHISTICATED STYLES

If you wanted a job in a bank, would you go for your job interview wearing a T-shirt, denim coveralls, boots, and a baseball cap on backward? No. You would market yourself for the job by looking the part.

What part are you applying for in a relationship? You are applying for the part of "romantic interest" in relationships with men.

A leading women's magazine conducted a nationwide study of men a number of years ago to determine which styles men like best: preppy, tailored, casual, sophisticated. Sophisticated clothing styles won. Sophisticated clothes are feminine, smart, a bit elegant, but not fussy.

A man does not want to be with a woman who is in clothing that is embarrassingly tight or scant. Remember, your clothing reveals your personality. To dress like a hooker gets you mistaken for a hooker, not for relationship material. Sophisticated, *tastefully* body-conscious clothing on a woman is just naturally attractive to a man.

Dress codes exist whether or not they are spelled out. People usually mingle with people who dress about the same way. It is an unspoken method of identifying your "type" of person. Do not confuse clothing style with cost. People can dress in the same style as their friends and yet not spend the same amount of money on clothes.

I prowled through stores all across the country while writing this book so I could tell you the national stores that carry clothes that fit relationship guidelines. Every one of these stores—J. C. Penney, Caché Contempo, The Limited, Talbots, Lillie Rubin, St. John, Mondi—provides great-looking clothes with man appeal (at different price levels) if you shop according to the love colors and love style guidelines.

Combining Your Wardrobe into Looks

All too often, women do not know how to combine clothes and accessories into different looks. Consequently, they end up looking the same, day after day. A man should see you in three distinctive looks.

Evening clothes should be worn with matching accessories, more eye makeup, and a glamorous hairstyle that is either loose or held with a clasp. Suits can be made dressy for evening with gold- or silver-toned shoes and belts. And gold- or silver-toned shoes and accessories go with absolutely anything.

Do not rely on black, beige, white, or brown accessories as neutral colors that will go with anything. They lack style and look bland and boring. A ''neutral'' can be any color you choose as your *coordinating color*. This year, perk up your wardrobe by choosing a bright color as your neutral. A belt, shoes, scarf, and handbag—all four—in the exact same shade of bright red.

They will go with everything. Bright red accessories look good with black, white, blue, yellow, and beige.

This separates you from every woman on the street with nothing but black, beige, or white accessories. You will love it.

Day looks and casual looks seem to be the most difficult for women. Below are three important guidelines for day dressing with style.

SOPHISTICATED	CASUAL	SOPHISTICATED/ CASUAL
Sleek hairstyle	Loose hairstyle	Sleek hairstyle with scarf
Smooth earrings	Loop earrings	Dangle or loop earrings
1 Bracelet	1–2 Bracelets	2 Bracelets
Buttoned jacket or scarf	Open jacket	Open jacket
Skirt, blouse, and scarf	Sweater or blouse, jeans	Turtleneck or silk shirt, slacks
Tinted stockings	No stockings	Opaque stockings
Mid to high heels	Flat to low heels	Flats

Be Superstitious About Your Clothing

Wear only happy clothes! If you have an outfit you paid a lot of money for but every time you wore it you had a bad time in it—sell it, donate it, consign it, throw it away, or burn it—but get rid of it!

What we mentally associate with something can affect our attitudes. If you have had unhappy experiences in certain clothing, you may subconsciously anticipate unhappiness whenever you put on that piece of clothing and may therefore actually attract another dull or unhappy experience.

No doubt you have clothes that, whenever you wore them, made you feel like a million dollars. People complimented you and you had a good time in them. Fill your closet with clothes like that. These are clothes that build your personal grooming power.

Top salespeople have lucky suits or lucky shirts or lucky ties. Many great historical figures had lucky clothes they had remade for years. Many superstar athletes and movie stars have lucky clothes.

Lucky clothes make you feel stronger. This is strictly mental—but then, it is in the mind that success and power happen. Be superstitious about your clothing.

MEN RESPOND TO HAPPINESS

The Attraction Principle

The Attraction Principle can bring more good your way than you can begin to imagine. The Attraction Principle is ... sparkling happiness. A woman who sparkles with happiness is a guaranteed man magnet.

Why do you want a relationship? You want a relationship to add happiness to your life, of course. It is the same for men. They want a woman who adds happiness to their lives.

If you are always complaining, "My parents did ..." and "My boss did ..." and "My kids are always ..." and "My neighbor can't ..." and on and on and on—a man knows you are misery in shoes and could never add happiness to his life!

Happiness Attracts More Love

What happens when you fall in love? You tingle with the excitement of happiness! But happiness itself attracts love. Learn to radiate happiness.

A woman who is happy generates a wattage of excitement about her. And studies have shown that people fall in love during excitement more than at any other time. When you generate your own wattage of excitement with happiness, you are a walking, talking love magnet.

How do you do that? You begin to say to yourself, "I am so excited about my life! I welcome all the love, beauty, and joy of life into me right now. And I appreciate the beauty of life around me. What a beautiful day—what a magnificent tree—what an interesting person— what a precious child!"

Even if you don't feel that way at first, choose to say it to yourself in order to rev up your wattage with the electricity of welcoming the joy and beauty of life into you.

I did this many times to wash my thoughts, cleanse my spirit, bathe my hopes, and fill myself with the electricity of life itself.

Happiness is a gift you give others, too. We can give happiness in a cheerful disposition, encouragement, and our own delight in life. Believe me, it is as much a gift as gold.

If *you* have happiness, people feel you must be someone special. They want to be near you—just to stand close to you—hoping it will somehow rub off on them. Unlike money, people do not mind receiving happiness from you as a gift that requires no return. They think you are wonderful! And you are.

Choose Happiness

What if you don't feel happy? Choose happiness. Express happiness. Fake it. Psychology shows that you can choose to smile as if you are happy and the act will actually result in a happier state of mind.

Learn to generate your own electrical excitement by learning how to sparkle with happiness everywhere you go. You can do it by:

- Walking just a bit faster than you usually do.
- Having an attitude of happy anticipation.
- Glancing about you as if you are looking for someone.
- You do not have to smile, but you should look as if you might any minute!

Sparkle makes the difference between one smile and another. Sparkle is personality projection.

7

How to Have Confidence

According to studies by Dr. Joyce Brothers, second to physical appearance, a man is most attracted to confidence in a woman.

Confidence does not mean you feel superior or egotistical. That is immature. Confidence means you know how to do something well. In this case, confidence means you know how to be you and to feel equal, genuine and comfortable with yourself, wherever you are.

Confidence shows in your body language. People believe your body language more than they do your words or your clothing signals. If there is a conflict between your words and your body language, people will believe your body language.

The following behavior is confidence body language that can change your body language signals into confident ones.

HOW TO SHOW CONFIDENCE

Posture

Your posture tells the world how to treat you from sight alone. People can tell if you are depressed, angry, excited, happy, feeling unsuccessful or feeling successful by your posture. Stand tall, shoulders back, back straight, and walk with your head up.

Standing Distance

A woman who lacks confidence will stand either too close or too far away while talking to people.

The most confident distance is sixteen to nineteen inches. Stand sixteen inches away when you're talking to men.

Buy a cheap measuring tape and practice standing sixteen inches from your wall. Then hold the tape at your side and walk up to the wall and stop when you think you are sixteen inches from it. Measure to see if you did it. Repeat several times. You will soon be able to stop in front of a man and know you are standing 16 inches from him, which is the distance that shows the most relationship confidence.

Full Body, Full Front

One sign of being intimidated, fearful, unattractively shy, and lacking confidence is to use your body as a shield by standing sideways and talking over your shoulder to a man.

To be a confident woman fully face a man with the front of your body.

Sidewalks, Hallways, Aisles

Women who are not confident will walk close to a building or to a wall, often with their eyes looking down.

To be a confident woman, walk center-most on the right-hand side of sidewalks, hallways, or aisles. As you walk, keep your chin up, your eyes casually looking about.

Doors

Women lacking confidence enter and leave buildings through doors that are closest to the wall.

As a confident woman, enter and exit department stores or office buildings through center doors.

Include Yourself

Women sometimes complain to me that they don't like to go to social functions alone because no one includes them when they are by themselves.

The truth is, it is a psychological impossibility for someone to make you feel included in a situation. When you don't feel included it is because of your own self-consciousness in the situation. But you can change that. *Let your body language say you are included, that you belong, without your having to say a word.*

Less confident women who join a circle of people talking to each other tend to stand just slightly behind the people on either side of them.

To show you are a confident woman, move *exactly* into the circle of people. Have your toes *exactly* in line with the toes of people on each side of you; and have your shoulders *exactly* in line with the shoulders of people on each side of you. This puts your face in their direct line of vision, so that you have included yourself in their eyes and their conversation.

You can hold your Perrier with both hands if that makes you feel better and simply sip and listen for a while to the conversation with an alert attention. Your body language says you belong, and people will treat you according to your body language.

You do not have to smile; just look alert, interested, and patient until an opportunity opens for you to say something.

Restaurants and Coffee Shops

A less confident woman who is alone will sit with her back to the action of the room. Her body language says, "Don't bother me."

A confident woman will choose to sit at a centrally located table where she is facing the action of the room. She can see everybody and everybody can see her. Her choice of seating invites by sending an open, receptive message. Her body language in this choice of seating says, "I'm ready for relationships!"

Even if I moved the less confident lady to the table that faces everyone, she would feel so self-conscious that she would fill all the chairs at her table with her handbag, briefcase, store purchases, and umbrella.

By doing that, she is once again sending closed, shut-down messages and signals "I am not ready for relationships."

No Isolation Devices

A less confident lady may bury her head in a book or, worse yet, she may put on earphones. Do not do this. Books can be a prop if you only scan and turn pages, slowly, pausing to look up at people around you as you turn each page.

Casual Eye Contact

When you are in a restaurant, have confident eye contact. This is casual, noninvasive eye contact with people around you.

Noninvasive eye contact is a very smooth, traveling eye movement that is eye-to-eye with each person for only half a second as it smoothly moves to the next person. It is a bit like scanning, as if you are simply looking around and you are interested in everything around you.

Of course, think your magic words so that your face has an energy of simmering excitement to it!

Anticipation, Not Smile

Do not sit there with a big smile on your face. Instead, have a look of anticipation of everything good that you know is there.

Personality

Bottom line, a man may be attracted to you physically, but it will be your personality that clinches his interest in making a date. If you are alone, how can he see your personality?

Let a man see your personality as you interact with the server who says to you, "May I take your order?"

Let us say you have only enough money for a cup of coffee. But if all you say is "Coffee," that shows no personality! No one will even notice it.

Instead, when the server approaches and says, "May I help you?" I want you to light up and ask, "What kinds of wonderful desserts do you have?"—or whatever you can get emotional about (I get emotional about desserts).

He or she may simply hand you a dessert menu, but don't let the server get away. Use the menu as a prop. Begin to ask the server questions about every dessert on the menu. And whatever you are told—respond to it!

> YOU: "The pecan pie—is it Southern pecan pie, made with molasses?"
>
> SERVER: "I don't really know, but people tell me it's good."
>
> YOU: "I am sure it is. What about the Irish whiskey cake? Is it real Irish whiskey cake like Bailey's Irish Whiskey cake?"

You get the idea. In other words, you show lots and lots of personality—and at some point, I don't care what the server says, laugh! Laughter is appealing and attention-getting if it isn't too loud.

HOW TO BE APPROACHABLE

This restaurant lesson is a very important one for learning how to express your personality with people around you because interacting pleasurably with people around you makes you approachable to an onlooker.

Interact with people everywhere you go. Talk to people of all ages in a casual, upbeat way that does not get personal.

The way to avoid getting personal in conversation with people is to talk about something you have in common in your surroundings, not about yourself and not about them.

Small comments to someone next to you about the weather, about the elevator, about the building, about the plants growing in the corner, about the season . . . these are nonthreatening topics that create small bright spots of interaction throughout your day—several times an hour with several people. This simple ability is one of the most important ways to create the charisma that makes you approachable.

Keep at it. Practice interacting casually every day, everywhere, and it will begin to work more easily and magnetically for you. Talk to women, too. Life is meant to be lived richly and fully with both sexes. The more fully you enjoy one sex, the greater the overflow you will have into the other sex.

8

Secret Flirting Techniques

The message of flirting is, "I am ready for relationships!" Flirting is the courtship body language signaling that you are ready for men, for dating, for love, for marriage—for the risk of relationships—ready for love's exciting adventure!

"I am ready for relationship*s*!" Plural. "But, Ginie," you plead, "I only need one man."

Wrong. You need choices.

If your message is "I am ready for *a* relationship" then you are not flirting, you are hunting. Hunting is too hungry. You come across as desperate. Men sense it and shun you. They can tell the difference.

Flirting is the readiness to enjoy many different men on many different levels. Flirting is readiness for the now whether it leads anywhere or not. Flirting is a readiness that enjoys a relationship without having to put a destination on it. Flirting is strictly a no-strings-attached freedom for both people who are enjoying each other that moment. Flirting creates possibilities for the future.

ARE YOU *REALLY* READY FOR RELATIONSHIPS?

A three-year-old child may want to read like her big sister. She may throw tantrums and cry because her big sister can read a book. She may want to *know how* to read, but that doesn't mean she is ready to *learn how* to read.

In education there is something known as the readiness factor. When a child is ready to learn how to read, she begins recognizing symbols and asking questions about letters. This is known as readiness behavior.

The same thing is true in relationships. There is a big difference between wanting relationships and being ready for relationships.

When a woman is really ready for marriage, she shows it by exhibiting certain readiness behaviors, known as flirting. She is open and receptive to many relationships with many different men on many different levels of enjoyment. But are you? Are you, in fact, *really* ready for relationships? There are eight very important questions for you to answer that can determine a lot about your readiness level.

Question #1:
What kinds of excuses are you giving yourself to justify not having the relationships you want?

If you do not feel satisfied with your relationship life, what kinds of excuses are you hiding behind? In my constant travels, giving seminars and private one-on-one consultations throughout the United States and Canada these many years, I have heard every excuse anyone can come up with. The most common excuses are:

- "I'm too old . . ." (I have even heard this from people who are thirty!) I have a client in her mid-sixties who married two years ago. She took the risk (and decided not to hide behind excuses). You can learn as she did that love has no age limit.

- "I have a handicap . . ." PBS did a follow-up on the Thalidomide babies. These were babies born in the 1960s whose mothers had been given Thalidomide while they were pregnant. The children were born without some of their limbs—arms or legs. Those children are adults now, and the interesting fact to me is that those who didn't use their handicap as an excuse are happily married and have children.

- "If I were better educated . . ." One of my clients, who is a Harvard graduate, said, "Maybe if I just learn French . . ." "Sweetheart," I said gently to her, "believe me, learning French will not make you one bit more lovable—unless you live in France."

- "I have too many children . . ." A student of my seminars had five small children. She decided not to use them as an excuse and she is very happily married today.

- "If I could just lose fifteen pounds . . ."

- "I'm not good-looking enough . . ."

- "If I made more money . . ."

If you sat in front of the Marriage License Bureau every day from eight A.M until five P.M. for two weeks, you would see couples coming in for marriage licenses and you would see plenty of women who are a lot more than fifteen pounds overweight, women who are a lot older than you, women with a greater handicap than yours, women who are not as pretty as you, women who are less educated than you, women who have less money than you, women who have more children than you—in other words, the women who are getting married are those who refuse to give themselves an excuse *not* to have relationships. Excuses are powerful deterrents.

Question #2:
*Do you really want to go forward
or do you really want to go back?*

You have probably had a really great relationship at some point in your life. A relationship in which a particular man was e-v-e-r-y-t-h-i-n-g you wanted. He totally fulfilled and satisfied your soul and made you want even more. Clearly, you had found your soulmate. He was "The One." He was perfect, you were perfect, the relationship was exhilarating and perfect . . . and yet . . . for some reason he is not in your life today.

And now you ask yourself, "What's wrong with me? I was able to have such a great relationship back then, and I can't get anything going now . . . what's wrong with me?"

There is nothing *wrong* with you. It is just that you have one hand reaching out to the future, wanting to go forward into new relationships, and you have one hand reaching back into the past, holding on to a memory.

With your hands reaching in opposite directions of desire, you are stuck in the middle. You cannot move in either direction—you can't go forward because you can't let go of the past, and you can't let go of the future because you have nothing to go back to. So emotionally, you can't go anywhere. You are stuck. It's an emotional tug-of-war that you can't win.

To get unstuck, you must face this fact: There will never be another man like him again. Never again in your life. The relationship you had with him will never happen again. The relationship is over. Gone forever. It is dead to your life. No man will ever make you feel the way he did. Therefore, when you find yourself saying "Well, Bill is nice, but he doesn't make me feel the way Tom did" or "Bill doesn't kiss like Tom," you are absolutely right! No one will ever duplicate what you and Tom had together.

And that is *good*! No matter how wonderful the memory seems, if you really could get another Tom, you would be living your life in reruns and each relationship would end up the same way as the one with Tom, with your heart broken.

You do not need another Tom. Begin to say that and say it until you realize the truth of it and say it until you mean it.

When you get to the point when you can turn and look at the memory, stare it down, and truthfully say, "If I could have you back *now*, I wouldn't. And not to spite you, not out of pride, but because I have already tried it; and no matter what I tell myself, it would end up the same way.

"No, I would not have it back. What I want is a relationship that is all brand-new—something completely different, something I have never experienced before."

Then, you will feel the weight of the past relationship snap and fall away, freeing you—and you will move forward quickly and easily into new relationships.

WHAT FLIRTING IS NOT

Sandra met Jim at the opening of his new country-western club. He was a tall, handsome man, surrounded by people congratulating him on the success of his opening night. He winked and smiled at her, asking, "What's your name?"

"Sandra," she answered, but before he could say anything else, other newcomers demanded his attention. Throughout the night, Sandra noticed he always smiled when he saw her and his eyes lingered with interest. She knew something special had begun between them.

Sandra later learned from a bartender that Jim came to his country-western club only on Thursday nights. And every Thursday night, Sandra showed up at his club. There were always people around him, but everytime he saw her he smiled with his usual, lingering eye contact.

Sandra was filled with excitement everytime their eyes met. She knew he was feeling what she was feeling. If only he weren't so shy, she thought. If only he knew how to break the ice with her—or if she only knew how to break the ice with him. "Next Thursday," she kept telling herself each time she left. "Next Thursday he will ask me to dance or talk to me."

So, every Thursday night for more than eleven years, Sandra went to his country-western club and flirted with him. *This is a true story.* During that time, he got married, had a child, got divorced, got married again, got divorced again. But he didn't know how to break the ice with Sandra? Not true. She had created a fantasy relationship out of a flirtation. Unfortunately, it is not all that uncommon. I meet intelligent, successful women and men all the time who are not savvy on this point.

It may have been easier for Sandra to deceive herself with the exciting tease of a fantasy relationship through flirtation than to deal with the complexities of actual relationships with him or with other men.

Why did he flirt with her? He thought she was cute and he could tell she liked him, but he had other things going on in his life.

Eight out of ten men who flirt with you are just flirting. They compliment your attractiveness with a flirtation, but that doesn't obligate them to feel a personal interest in getting to know you.

Nature designed flirting that way. Accept it and relish it. Flirting is a feather-light compliment or a possible interest. Flirting is *not* a relationship. So what's wrong with a compliment? Who couldn't use a flirtatious compliment now and then? Learn to accept it as that and preen—it means you are doing well and being noticed by men!

How will you know if it is just a compliment or a possible interest? If it is a possible interest there will be follow-up for a cup of coffee or a date. Make a promise with yourself that until you and a man actually have a date together, you and he are "just flirting"—and that's okay.

If you want more than flirtation but he doesn't cross the line, then you may have to be the one to ask him out or be willing to stop flirting with him and let him go.

PLAY THE ODDS FOR FLIRTING SUCCESS

You also must understand the power of numbers in flirting. On average, you will have to interact with fifty men in order to meet three men who will even be interested or available. Out of the three men who are interested, only one man stands a 50 percent chance of becoming a relationship.

If you are only meeting fifty new men a year, you are in slo-o-ow motion! Very slow motion.

You can meet fifty new men a week. You can interact with ten new men a day, five days a week on the weekdays and double up on the weekends—now that's putting some action in your life! Eventually, I hope you will flirt with fifty men a day.

What I want you to understand is that it's a numbers game. There is no escaping the sorting process in relationships, and the more numbers you have to work with, the sooner you find what you want.

Don't feel bad about it—feel glad! That means you have a level playing field. Frankly, it doesn't matter if it is you or Kim Basinger, the numbers are the same.

Sure, a beautiful woman may attract more immediate attention, and she may meet fifty men faster, but it still takes the same number.

EVERYTHING YOU DO IS A LEARNED SKILL

Think about it. Even cooking doesn't come naturally. And just because you have all the ingredients in the kitchen doesn't mean you know how to cook. Likewise, you can have all the best natural assets in the world, but that doesn't mean you know how to be successful with men. It takes skills.

One day I realized that everything you do from the time you wake up in the morning until you go to sleep at night is a learned skill.

You have forgotten learning some of the skills you now take for granted. Everything from potty training to bathing yourself, brushing your teeth, talking, listening, dressing yourself, grooming and adorning yourself, cooking and using utensils to feed yourself—all are learned skills.

You get a paycheck at the end of every month for what? For the learned skills you perform on your job. A high school or college diploma certifies your learned skills in a discipline. And you are required to have a license for the learned skills of driving a car or selling real estate or performing surgery. Skills make life more effective for us. The more skills you have, the more control you have over your life.

Flirting and meeting men are learned skills. When the skill is effective, then your life in that area is effective, satisfying, functioning well, and you are happy with it. This means that you are more in control of your life than you even know.

Successful relationships are not luck! They are a matter of numbers, practice, and skills. Numbers create practice, which creates skills. That is your chain link for success in anything in life, including relationships.

WHEN AND WHERE TO FLIRT

You want to flirt just about everywhere you go! Standing in any line and in waiting rooms, lobbies, elevators, supermarkets, car washes, laundries, convenience stores, banks, ATM machines, fast-food restaurants, clubs, parties, entering or leaving buildings, and malls.

OFF-LIMITS FLIRTING

The one place you must not flirt is at work. Sexual harassment is real. Oh, I know you don't intend your flirting as sexual harassment of a man, but if he works for you or under you, he could feel a subtle pressure, psychologically, about your interest in him that makes him feel obligated, even though he isn't interested. It could cause him to worry about his job. No one should dread going to work because of an implied sexual pressure from a co-worker.

Do not think I say this for political correctness. This is a reality. Men can take women to court for sexual harassment just as women take men to court.

The flip side of it is that your flirting can also invite sexual harassment toward you by someone in your office. Either way, it is not worth the hassles you could find yourself in. Just don't flirt during working hours.

If someone works in your building but not for your company, that is a different matter. Neither of you feels your livelihood is at stake due to sexual pressure. The flirtation does not affect either of your jobs.

If someone in your company wants to date you, give it serious thought. Does your job mean a lot to you? Can you replace it easily? If a relationship actually develops between you and this person, will it affect either of you on the job? If you have a date with this person and he never asks you out again, will it bother you?

Will this man have any say in your career advancement? If so, and if you are dating and you do not advance in your career, how will you feel about it? If you and he stop seeing each other and you do not advance in your career, will you think it is personal on his part?

There is a lot to consider before leaping into a relationship with a co-worker or a boss. It can be worth it, of course, if marriage results, but count the cost first—and accept responsibility for the outcome.

FLIRTING IS AN OPEN AND RECEPTIVE BODY LANGUAGE

Would you try to go into a store that had Out of Business or Closed signs pasted over the windows and doors? Of course not. There is nothing in there for you.

Men will not approach a woman who projects a message like that, either. There is nothing there for them. She isn't open for a relationship, just as the store isn't open for business.

Mind you, a woman may think she is open for a relationship because she inwardly wants one. She may not know she is sending closed or fearful signals. Flirting is the way a woman sends open, receptive signals that market her for relationships.

Marketing yourself for relationships through flirting tells men you are available without saying a word.

Your body language has to say you are open for relationship business.

MAN-MAGNET FLIRTING

The purpose for flirting, of course, is to meet more men. Therefore, you will be most effective if you keep your flirting appropriate to the situation and if you use techniques that are compatible with your real personality. Even so, take a few risks to make your relationship life more exciting—whether you are a shy flirt or a teasing flirt (who is not shy)!

A shy woman needs techniques that seem natural and will not embarrass her if they don't work.

Notes for the Shy Flirt. You don't have to do anything embarrassing or phony to flirt. For a shy person, flirting has more to do with intent than with technique. *Simple interaction can be flirting.*

Rely on average, everyday interactions as you do with your friends—but apply these interactions to men you want to meet and do so in a manner that seems upbeat.

A shy woman can interact with a man in a natural, no-frills way— thus opening the door for possibilities between them—by asking simple, everyday questions she would ask her mother. That way, if he shows no interest, she hasn't lost face because her question was not forward.

Teasing Flirting

"Maybe" is the undercurrent to everything a teasing flirt does. "Maybe" is sexier than "Yes" or "No." "Maybe" is the tease.

A tease is flirting and she doesn't care who knows it. She likes relationships and she isn't ashamed of it. She considers it healthy—and it is! And she fully enjoys it.

Even if you are not a teasing flirt, learn what she does and you may find an occasion when you can use some of the teasing techniques.

A teasing flirt uses lots of eye contact, accentuated courtship body language, and sexy walks. In fact, let's start with sexy stance and sexy walks.

The Fertility Curve. The way a woman carries herself when she is standing or walking conveys a very important message to men on a subliminal level. In fact, the most powerful courtship body language is the curve of your spine. To create the fertility curve, do the following:

- Stand against a wall with the following points of your body touching the wall:
  - **head**, keeping your chin level, not up
  - **shoulders**, keeping them back but not stiff
  - elbows, but not hands
  - **butt**
  - **calves**, if possible
  - **heels**
- Widen the distance between your belly button and your ribcage. Wider.
- Holding this stance, put one hand on the base of your spine and push gently in, making a deep curve at the base of your spine. Replace your elbow against the wall.
- Step away from the wall. Perfect!!!

This particular curve of a woman's spine begins to form when she enters puberty. Her hormones send a new message to her brain, which in turn sends a new message to her spine to arch her shoulders and to curve in deeply just above her hips.

The curve, designed by nature, is a signal to men that a woman has now reached the age of fertility, which is why I named it the fertility curve.

Older men do not prefer younger women because they are younger. They may think that is why they like them, but it isn't. It is that a younger woman naturally has the deep curve in her spine.

As a woman ages, she loses bone mass and her body slowly sinks into a slump of shoulders, rounding down to her hips. This does not signal a mating invitation.

But older women can get the same response of interest from men as many of the younger women if they learn to duplicate the mating signal by using the fertility curve.

It is the curve of her spine, and not the size of a woman's bust or her hips or her thighs, that a man responds to. Christy Brinkley won fame in the swimsuit issue of *Sports Illustrated* but if she had auditioned wearing the same swimsuit, standing slumped over, her back in a hunched curve from her shoulders to her hips, she would not have been chosen for the magazine.

And yet she would have had the same bust measurement, the same hip size, the same slender thighs, the same lovely face. What made her sexy in the swimsuit? Her spine!

In flamenco dancing, which is a dance that represents seduction, the deeply arched back in the dancer is a deliberate part of the dance, to emphasize the dance of courtship and mating between men and women.

When a woman of any age is standing or walking, she should always stand with her fertility curve in full effect!

Sultry Vamp Walk. With your fertility curve in force, pretend you are walking on a straight line. Step one foot directly in front of the other foot, leading with your hips into long, sultry strides. Do not move your upper body. Keep your arms loose and relaxed at your sides. Lead with your hips. Pretend you are Kathleen Turner in *Body Heat.*

Move-Over-Marilyn-Monroe Walk. Again, pretend you are walking on a straight line. Fertility curve ready. Now, step one foot directly in front of the other foot, taking teeny, tiny steps, very quickly, one after the other. This creates a cute wiggle.

Your Natural Walk, Enhanced. Most of the time, rely on your natural gait, only walk just a bit faster to get your energy up. Use your fertility curve, think your magic words—*Men are wonderful, I am wonderful, sex is wonderful*—and you will be a dynamo!

Whichever walk you choose, be sure that while walking you choose to like everything around you, everything you see.

This is important, because if you are looking at things and thinking "What a stunning display" or "Wow! What a great color for a dress," your face will be filled with a lively energy of anticipation and joy.

And it is the energy and life in a woman's face that men respond to and consider beautiful. Positive thoughts create energy. You even walk faster.

If you are looking around and thinking "What an ugly display" or "Yuk! What a color for a dress," your face turns sour, your eyes dull. Negative thoughts kill energy. Your walk will even slow down. Try it. You'll see.

As you walk, flirt with just about every man who is past puberty and still kicking! Well . . . at least past eighteen and not senile, is that better? And, of course, be sure you are always in safe locations.

Sitting Sexy. When a woman crosses her leg over her knee, she is simply comfortable. But the higher she crosses the leg on her thigh, the more interested she is in men. Sitting this way forces her spine automatically into the fertility curve.

This style of leg-crossing is just plain prettier, too. From the front, your legs look shaplier, sleeker, sexier. It is the most flattering way a woman can show off her body, her silhouette, and her legs.

This style of sitting is feminine as well as sensuous if a woman stays aware of her skirtline. Keep your skirt discreet.

The Importance of Eye Contact. Eye contact is a nonverbal cue of availability. If your eye contact briefly "locks" with a man's, you are both signaling availibility for a relationship. If one of you looks away before the eye contact locks, that person is sending a not-available signal. If available, you and he look away *after* the brief lock.

Before You Make Eye Contact. When you look at a man, the content of your eye contact is most important. If you have a quizzical look in your eyes, the man will wonder if something is wrong with him— or you! If you have an overly serious look in your eyes, you could look threatening and scare the daylights out of him.

But, if you are thinking *Men are wonderful, I am wonderful, sex is wonderful!* you will have an expression of delight in your eyes. And that is perfect for the eye content of flirting.

Timing Your Eye Contact. Flirting instructors have adopted my method of timing eye contact in a number of seconds (the ''lock''), then looking away. Timing your eye contact is very important.

A one-second eye contact is seldom long enough. Six seconds is usually too much. I give preferred numbers for each exercise below. However, find a range between one and six seconds that is comfortable for you to sustain eye contact with a new man.

Shy Flirt Eye Contact. A shy woman tends to look away before the lock, thereby signaling she is not available, when she really is. Naturally, then, she has to find a way to show interest in a man with her eyes in a way that is comfortable to her.

A shy woman can easily master my low-key eye contact technique: She should immediately glance back, twice, at a man if she has looked away too quickly. The double-back glances help compensate for missing the all-important brief ''lock.'' If she can quickly and actively think *men are wonderful, I am wonderful, sex is wonderful,* the impact will be great.

Teasing Flirt Eye Contact While Seated or Standing. Think your magic words to rev up energy. Look directly into a man's eyes. On the count of three, keeping your eyes locked on his, turn your head to the side, then on the count of four, let your eyes follow your face. Don't glance back. Remember: Look, lock, look away.

Teasing Flirt Eye Contact While Walking. Look directly into his eyes for two full seconds. Move your face away on the second count, keeping your eyes locked to the count of two; then let your eyes slide to the front. Look, lock, look away.

Advanced Flirting Eye Contact. As you pass a man, think the words "I might go to bed with you!" (don't say it, think it) as you glance at him and look away. You have no intention of going to bed with him, but it's a great test of ESP. When he does a double-take, you'll swear ESP is real.

Winking. There are different winking styles. Some women have mastered the deep, slow wink; others prefer the quick wink. Either is fine, depending on how you feel at the time.

Indiscriminate Winking. When you are in a crowded room, look to the general right of the room, give a big smile, and wink! Look into the center of the room, give a big smile, and wink! Look to the left of the room, give a big smile, and wink! And see who thinks it was for him!

High-Interest Winking. Focus on a man who is not looking at you. When he looks up and sees you, give a big smile and wink, then turn completely away from him.

Smiling. Smiles go with winks, but you can seem more intense if you wink without a smile. Whether or not you smile, move your attention smoothly away from a man as soon as you have winked.

Sizzling Excitement. Smiling is not necessary. Fill your face with anticipation and a sense of excitement and you won't need to smile. The energy in your face will have the greatest impact. Have an expression of sizzling excitement just below the surface.

When your face is filled with energy and interest, a smile is very close at hand if someone smiles at you or if something delights you.

No-flinch Staring. Focus on a man who is not looking at you. Think your magic words as you look at him, but do not smile. When he looks up at you, do not smile, do not waver, do not flinch. Just stare.

Sudden Bold Staring. You have been trying to get a certain man to notice you all night long, to no avail. Suddenly, you stand up, whirl around, put your hands on your hips, bend toward him from the waist, and smile and stare, and smile and stare, and smile and stare!

Abruptly turn back around, sit down, and ignore him the rest of the time you are there. Everyone in the room might know what you are doing, but you shouldn't care! That has to be your attitude if you want to carry this off.

One man was so taken by the woman who did this to him that when she left (with her date!) shortly after her sudden bold stare, he went to a lot of trouble to track down who she was and called her.

Stare-Wink-Stare. Stare at a man, and when he sees you, wink, and continue to stare.

Crowding. Each of us is surrounded by an invisible bubble of space that is our individual territory. This bubble of space is our own personal real estate, and we get quite territorial about it if someone stands too close to us.

So that is exactly what you do! You quietly invade a man's space as if by accident until he notices you. Only you invade it with your back to him. You talk to someone else while you take a slight step backward into his space. He will step back from you.

After a minute, as you continue conversing with someone and sipping your coffee or cocktail, you step back against him, again.

He steps back again. After a pause, you step back into his space once more.

This continues until he runs out of room and your back is practically hugging up against him.

At this point, there are three options:

1.   He may say something—"Ahem! Excuse me, but . . ." and you respond "Oh, excuse me. Uhm, my name is Betsy . . . What is your name?"

2.   You step back, bumping into him, suddenly notice yourself, and turn to say, "Oh, my goodness, excuse me [then pause and smile slightly] . . . My name is Betsy. What is your name?"

3. You may just step on his foot to create a stronger reason to say something. "Oh, my gosh! Sorry! I know that hurts. Here, let me treat you to another cup of coffee [drink]. . . . My name is Betsy. What is your name?"

Crowding with a Stare. (Only for the boldest of the bold.) Facing a man and staring him in the eyes, you move toward him, into his bubble of space. He steps back, you step forward, staring. You may sip your coffee, but you keep your eye contact and your pace of advancing as he retreats.

Force him to say something first by simply continuing your crowding and staring. No matter what he says (unless it is crude and offensive), respond by saying, "I was hoping you would say that. My name is Betsy. What is yours?"

For instance, he may look exasperated and say, "Uh, please . . ." You say, "I was hoping you would say that. My name is Betsy. What is yours?" If, instead, he says something rude, just walk off.

You can get away with being bold as long as you don't come across in a square-shouldered way, like Hulk Hogan in World Championship Wrestling—about to toss him down and bounce off his chest!

You have to be a saucy little charmer to carry this off, but if you can, it's fun.

Teasing Comments. Teasing comments are a form of verbal play. They are cheerful comments you make about whatever a man is: looking at, leaning against, standing next to, doing, sharing in the environment with you, or sharing in the world with you.

You tease by saying something obviously not true as if it is. What you say does not have to be funny, only said in a fun manner that invites response in a light, nonthreatening way.

One day I saw a woman in a tobacco shop sniffing cherry pipe tobacco. A gentleman in the back of the store noticed her, walked closer to her, and said, "They charged me twenty-five cents to do that."

Now, obviously, no one charged him twenty-five cents to sniff the tobacco. He was teasing.

The woman, still holding the tobacco jar lid in her hand, smiled and asked, "So, will you pay my twenty-five cents for me?"

She is teasing, too. This is verbal play, a charming interaction, gentle flirting.

I once saw a gentleman holding a Liz Claiborne shopping bag.

"So, you are Liz Claiborne!" I said to him in a fun tone.

He glanced down at the bag, then back up at me, and matching my fun tone, said, "Why, yes, I am. I'll bet I'm not at all what you expected. What's your name?" It was a great response. Hats off to him!

Three-Squeeze Handshaking. A man approaches you and you extend your right hand for a handshake.

- Fold your left hand over the back of his hand, forming a double-clasp. Squeeze both your hands while shaking his hand.
- Quickly move your left hand just above his wrist and squeeze both hands again, while still shaking hands.
- Return to the double-clasp and squeeze both hands one more time as the handshake ends!

You can complete this three-step handshake in five seconds! It is well worth practicing. It is very warm and men remember it.

Touching. Be careful where you touch. Don't be a fawning toucher, a backslapper, or an affectionate mauler. Use the three-squeeze handshake, then continue holding his hand in the final double clasp longer while you talk.

When the handclasp breaks, keep your hands off the person until the conversation ends. At that time, you can shake hands again and walk away.

Or you can reach out and grasp the person's shoulder, hand, or forearm as you sum up your final comment.

Or you can reach out and pat the person on the arm or back as you turn away with final remarks.

9

Add Men and Romance to Your Daily Life

Now that you know the power of magic words, now that you know how to dress, how to be confident, and how to flirt, you are ready to get men into your life.

PLACES

One of the most common questions women ask me is, "Where can I go to meet men?" Every single time, without exception, I have glanced around us and we were outnumbered by men.

"What about these men?" I ask.

The women are always surprised when I ask that. Looking around, they seem to feel that it is impossible to meet the man standing at the elevator, reading the paper, rummaging through his briefcase that is balanced precariously on his knee, or the man sipping coffee at the next table.

There is a myth in our society that there is a place where all the meetable, datable, single, and available men hang out. And if you can just learn the name of this place, you'll go get yours.

You are single and available right now. You are single and available when you fill up your car with gas. You are single and available when you dash into the convenience store to buy milk. You are single and available when you pick up your clothes from the cleaner's. You are single and available when you browse a card shop for a friend's birthday.

You are single and available as you push your shopping cart down the supermarket aisle. You are single and available as you enter your synagogue or church or other place of worship. You are single and available when you jog, park your car, stop at a stop light, or wait for an elevator. You are single and available everywhere you go—and that is exactly how it is with single and available men.

All these normal, everyday places you go in your day-to-day life are exactly the places to meet men! Everywhere! There is no shortage of men to meet.

You can see that meeting men these various ways enables you to meet them everywhere. And that's the kind of power you want to have.

Temporary Jobs

Working as a temp brings you into contact with new people. Some of the jobs may not be very exciting and may be menial; nevertheless, it can be fun to go to a different job everyday in a different office in a different part of town where there are new people, new friends to make, new men to meet.

One year, I did this and found it to be quite interesting. Sometimes I did it for the week or two I had as vacation. The work wasn't as demanding as my usual job, and just doing something different was restful. It also provided a small extra income and new men to date, new friends to enjoy.

On the Sidewalk

An interesting-looking man is about to pass you on the sidewalk, going in the opposite direction. Thinking quickly, you remember that a Starbucks coffeehouse is at the end of the block in the direction he is heading. Since you are walking in the opposite direction, you say, ''Excuse me, do you know if Starbucks is nearby?''

Of course, there is always the possibility that he is from out of town or really doesn't know where the store you've asked about is, but your chances are good that he does business in the vicinity and that he does know where it is.

"Sure," he says. "Starbucks is at the end of this block, to the right. You are going the wrong way."

"Oh, I just came from that direction and I didn't see it. Since you are going that way, do you mind pointing it out to me?"

During the walk to the end of the block, you and he can converse lightly about the day, about Starbucks, about coffee, about the area. Do not sound eager. Once he points out the coffeehouse to you, thank him and—if you have the courage—offer to buy him a cup of coffee as a thank-you.

If you don't have the courage to offer to buy him coffee, then as you are walking with him, get one of your cards out of your handbag. When he points the way to Starbucks, simply hand him your card and say, "Thank you very much. I hope I see you again sometime," and walk away.

Make Comments. This is a wonderful technique, not only for a shy woman but for anyone. Cultivate this technique and you will be a bright spot in the lives of many people!

The mechanics of this flirtation method work like this: You are walking along when you see a man who is looking at something, doing something, leaning against something, or standing next to something.

As you approach him, slow down but *do not stop.* As you pass, make a cheerful comment about whatever he is involved with at that moment.

For example: You walk into a card shop and see a man on one aisle looking at a greeting card. You walk down his aisle, slow down as you near him, but do not stop, and cheerfully say, "I sent that card to my brother and he just loved it!" as you pass, continuing to walk down the aisle. Don't look back. Just round the corner and say something in a cheerful tone to the salesperson.

Now, the man with the card is standing there, and he thinks "What???" And if he is available for a relationship, he loves it!

Do not be concerned whether or not he is available for a relationship. After all, you are not interacting just with men you want to meet. You are casually interacting with just about everyone. The purpose of your comment is to tap his interest to see if he is available for a possible relationship.

Inside each of us, whenever we are not in a relationship or in a fulfilling relationship, there is a core of isolation. Our hearts feel trapped inside, a bit like the butterfly tapping its wings, trying to break out of its cocoon. And we secretly long for someone to gently violate our isolation and let us out.

Gently. You see, if you stop to talk to the man, he may feel imposed upon and will want to flee. He will be silently thinking, "Go away!" If you merely make a comment and keep moving, you have opened the door of opportunity for him to make the next move if he is available.

A woman in California contacted me after learning this in my flirting seminar. "Ginie," she said, "I have lived in a singles area for a number of years and shopped at the supermarket where a lot of women have met men and started dating them. Still, I had never had a dating relationship start from the men I met there—and now I know why.

"It was because I would see men and stop and talk to them. They would finally make an excuse and move on.

"After your seminar, I went to the supermarket and I began just to make comments to men about the produce as I passed and, without stopping, I continued to push my cart through the aisle. And, surely enough, here they would come down another aisle to talk to me and to get my number! I have been dating several men I met there. The key was what you said about not stopping."

Exchange Cards. If you have met someone you would like to see more of, and he doesn't ask for your name, number, or card, then—with a big smile—ask if he has a card while you reach into your handbag to get yours. If he says he doesn't have a card, keep smiling and hand your card to him, saying, "Here is my card. I enjoyed talking to you and I look forward to seeing you again sometime." Do not wait for his response, just turn and go!

You can use business cards, but also have personal cards made with only your name and telephone number (voice mail, if you like). You can put "tennis enthusiast" or "chocolate chip cookie lover" under your name—or anything charming. Don't put suggestive comments like "hot lips."

Waiting Rooms

Always sit down next to a man. Always. This is to keep yourself aware of men, aware of choosing men, and it keeps your body comfortable with the closeness of a man.

Some women say, "But what if he's married?" Well, what if he is? You are only sitting down. You can't avoid sitting down next to a man because you are worried that he might be married. If so, you are living from avoidance motivation. If he is married, you'll find that out.

However, you may not end up talking to him at all. You are just choosing to be bodily close to men as often as possible, even casually.

Choosing always to sit and to stand close to men is a far more important choice than you can imagine for keeping your magnetism with men.

When you sit down next to a man, don't say anything unless he looks up at you. Then, only smile or say "Hello" and seem polite but interested in something else—getting seated, locating a magazine. Do not seem directly interested in him. As you sit down, turn your attention to putting your keys into your purse and settling into your chair.

If he doesn't look up at you, don't be deterred. Don't say anything, either. Just settle in, putting away your keys and selecting a magazine or paper from the waiting room table.

Cross your legs toward him and angle your body slightly toward him. This is a receptive body language signal. Don't react to a man's negative body language. You stay in control with your open, receptive body language. Even if he shifts away from you, don't change your body signals.

However, as long as his body language is turned away from you, remain silent and interested in what you are reading. This is no different from letting the neighborhood guard dog get used to you before you pet it. Keep your body receptive to him.

After a while he will get used to your being there. Without realizing what he is doing, he will reshift his body into a more comfortable position that accepts your presence. At that point, speak.

"Have you seen Dr. Goodteeth before?" you may ask, opening a casual conversation.

If the two of you talk long enough and enjoyably enough, and if you discern he isn't married, as you leave you can hand him your personal card, saying, "I enjoyed talking with you. Here is my card." Then leave.

Make Comments. What you say to a man is important only in that it should not be suggestive or sarcastic. But beyond that, anything you say is fine as long as it is upbeat, casual, and strictly for the moment. You are not trying to make anything out of it. You are not trying to make a relationship out of it. You don't have to say anything brilliant or clever.

Just make a general comment about the situation you share with him. You can simply say, "What a beautiful day!" If he doesn't say anything back, it is still a beautiful day and you haven't said anything wrong at all. It's his problem, not yours. Say it to another man, and another, later on.

You can also notice what he is carrying and make a comment about that. Do not give a compliment, however. Many men consider compliments as come-ons.

Ask Conversational Questions. If you ask questions, be sure they are not yes-or-no questions, which are conversational dead ends. Questions such as "Do you like..." or "Is ... good?" are dead-end yes-or-no questions.

Conversational questions are those that begin with *what, why,* and *how,* because they cannot be answered with a simple yes or no.

"What is your book about?"

"How did you get interested in the subject?"

A word of caution. Do not fire all these at once with someone or you do not have a conversation but an interrogation.

If you want a man to feel instant rapport with you, just listen closely while he talks. Then say "Oh, I see. You mean that..." and simply give a summary of what he just told you.

Always follow a man's answer with a comment of your own and then see if he is going to continue interacting. If not, you can ask another question, hear his comment, and say something in response.

Ask questions about time. Ask directions. And if you are new to a town or new to an area, admit it and ask about a good veterinarian, a convenient supermarket, a health food store, a dry cleaner's, and other establishments of interest to you.

Offer Help. If you see a man with his arms full, open a few doors for him. Ask if he has far to walk and discuss what he is carrying. If he drops something, pick it up and hand it to him, looking into his eyes in a nonmeaningful way. Be friendly and smile.

Whatever you picked up can be a conversation item. If it is wrapped, you can smile and say, "Hmmm, this is a mystery package."

If he is really overloaded, simply begin taking a few small items into your arms and say at the same time, "I'm going to help you. You can't manage this alone."

Be sure there are many people around. Stop before you get to his door. Do not go to his car. Do not go into his apartment or his office. Don't ever put yourself in any danger.

Keep your manner sincere. If nothing comes out of it, fine. You will have done a good deed for the day.

Share. If a popular restaurant has a long waiting line and a shortage of tables, offer to share yours with a gentleman who is also alone—or have the waiter ask a gentleman who is seated alone if it would be all right for you to join him since you are also alone and the waiting line is so long. If the answer is no, so what? If it's yes, stay low-key and pleasant throughout dinner.

If a man seems rushed and your cab arrives first, ask where he is going—and if it is in your direction, share your ride with him.

If there isn't much room to see an event—a parade or something else that is going on—share your space. You seem so superior to the average woman this way. You come across as aware, generous, kind, and thoughtful—as long as you make nothing of it. Stay focused on the event. Smile and be pleasant to the man but stay casual so you do not seem to have an ulterior motive. You already know not to seem suggestive.

Talk casually about the situation you are sharing and about the event. Let one topic simply lead to another without forcing anything. If talk moves smoothly, and when the event is over, if he doesn't ask for your name or number or to buy you coffee, ask for his card and give him yours. If nothing takes, you are still ahead in your development of personal charisma.

Give Only Appropriate Compliments. Compliments are tricky. Many men think a woman is coming on to them when she gives a compliment. Compliments about his physique, his eyes, or how handsome he is are out of line.

Still, there are times when a compliment is okay. Impersonal compliments are best, such as a compliment about something he is carrying. For example, "That's a nice-looking briefcase."

You can compliment his cologne. You can compliment a man's tie and occasionally his jewelry, as long as it doesn't seem that you are casing it! You can compliment his car if it is in complimentable condition. Even if it isn't, you can still compliment it as long as it comes across in a cute way that he can laugh about with you and not feel insulted.

Look Happily into a Man's Eyes, Smile, and Speak. Just say "Hi!" or "Hello!" Take your cue from his response and don't be concerned with his reaction. A simple hello, is not asking him to go to bed or to marry you.

Try this method in several situations per day. If a man says something, take it from there into small talk. If he doesn't, so what? Stay casual in your body language and say something cheerful to the very next person you see.

Be Direct. Being direct has a lot of appeal. True, it makes you more vulnerable to feeling rejected, and that can hurt, so you must be aware that you may feel rejected and be willing to accept it before you take this step.

But as long as you are sincere and straightforward without being forceful or suggestive or pushy, you can charm the daylights out of most decent men by simply handing him your card and saying "Excuse me, my name is Jane Doe. I noticed you when I came in and I would like to meet you."

When you make a statement like this, your next sentence depends on the situation. If you are in a social setting, you may add, "May I join you for a few minutes?" If he has no objection, join him and stay only a few minutes (I mean it!), then leave.

If you are both rushed to go elsewhere, your next sentence should be, "I am in a terrible rush and you clearly are, too. Do you have a card?'' If he gives you a card, ask, "Do you mind if I call you? We can have coffee sometime.''

If he seems to recoil from you or acts haughty or cold or indignant, ignore it. He may simply be taken off guard. Give him a chance to respond. After all, you have given him your card and he may call.

If he says nothing to you or if he says no or if he says drop dead or something worse, stay a lady and serenely go your way among other people.

If he is pleasant but says he is married or that he is involved or that he is not available or interested, don't persist. He has said no.

Just give a great big smile and say, "Well, I'm glad I asked, anyway. Bye,'' and move on.

This has been a very successful ploy for many women, especially those who are very busy and have to seize an opportunity at the moment.

A female physician did this with an attorney. He followed up and they got married. Another woman used this ploy at the airport as she was rushing to catch a plane. The man called a few days later and they began an exciting romance between cities.

If it doesn't work, what have you lost except a few minutes of possibly feeling embarrassed—but he is the one with the problem, not you. You didn't ask him to go to bed with you or to marry you. You simply expressed an interest in getting to know him. His loss.

Before you try this step—and I hope you do try it—be willing to take the risk of feeling rejected and not let it stop you from doing it again.

Ask His Assistance. If you are loaded down, ask a man (not another woman) to open doors for you, to help you carry a few things for a short distance, or to pick up something that you have dropped.

If you can get him to help you just a little distance with it, it gives you time to say something to him. When you put your load down, you can thank him and give him your card, asking if he works nearby.

Carry Props. Carry items that invite comments. A book on gardening, astronomy, or a controversial topic. Carry a camera and take pictures; you can say you are teaching yourself photography. Carry a racquetball bag and say that you are interested in the sport if anyone asks.

Use your imagination. Look around your home. See what you can come up with that isn't goofy and that can generate genuine interest.

Shopping Malls

When you go shopping is also a great time to practice and polish your flirting skills. In cities, this is especially true in chic high-tech-looking supermarkets or rustic-looking supermarkets that also have gourmet coffee beans, bakeries, and gourmet foods.

In most towns, large indoor malls have a social side to them. People shop, visit, browse, have lunch, and enjoy the upbeat atmosphere of the mall and the milling of people around them.

My husband and I conducted a study of men and women in malls in twenty-five major cities. We discovered that the biggest difference between men and women in malls has to do with elegant department stores.

Men do not hang out in fine department stores the way women do. Usually, a man enters such a department store for one of two reasons. He parked his car near the entrance of the store and so he enters to pass through the store to get to the mall! Or a man will go only to a certain area in a department store to find something specific. When he buys what he is looking for, he leaves.

Typically, a man does not browse in elegant department stores as a pastime, wandering from department to department in fascination. This is what women do, because to a woman a department store is Las Vegas! An elegant department store has everything we want in one building.

Men, on the other hand, prefer specialty stores in malls. They will be in Sharper Image, Brookstone, poster shops, tobacco shops (even if they don't smoke), knife shops, newsstands, bookstores, pet shops, and food plazas. These are all good places to practice flirting with men.

Help Him Out. If you see a man looking at women's items and seeming confused about what to buy, you can speak up and say, ''I think she will like that'' or ''You have good taste'' or ''Good choice.'' He may be buying the item for his mother, his sister, or, yes, a girlfriend . . . but so what? You are just practicing your interaction and flirting skills.

If you really want to pursue this, and if he responds positively to you, you can ask him to return the favor by helping you choose a fragrance for your father.

If you see a man who is trying on an oufit and evaluating it in front of a mirror, speak out and say, "That looks good on you" or "Yes, I vote for that one." Keep it positive and keep walking. Don't stop to chat. Go your way and don't try to make anything more of it. If he pursues it, fine. If he doesn't, fine. You are developing a wonderful, warm, responsive you—and the cumulative effect will ultimately pay off.

If you see him again later (and don't try to make it happen), ask him if he bought the outfit he was trying on.

Ask men what fragrance they are sniffing if you pass a counter where they are spritzing something on. Just stop and say, "Oooh, that smells good. What is it?" Then go.

Bookstores

Bookstores can be hotbeds of nice, intelligent men. Don't just hang out in the relationship or romance section. Get into the computer section, the music department, and business areas, as well as magazines.

Ask questions. "I am trying to learn about computers before I buy one. Do you know which books might be helpful?" Whatever he shows you, ask questions about it. You can look in the table of contents and ask questions from it. Give him your card as you walk away with one of the books (which you can turn in at the front or put back later).

Don't zero in on just one man, meet several. If the bookstore has a coffeehouse attached, you can suggest coffee.

Travel

Men who travel often have more derring-do because they feel freer away from their peers. They may be more responsive to your subtle approaches. Single travelers always secretly yearn for unexpected romance that may blossom into something meaningful. Therefore, they are looking for it.

When you are traveling, don't let down your guard on your looks.

Look good at all times. Always sit next to a man, stand next to a man, position yourself next to a man. Always. Casually chat. Respond.

Be Human. If you trip and fall or knock all the cans off the grocery shelf, or even if you break something, people will take their response cues from you.

Don't act angry or humiliated. Get up with dignity, chuckling, straighten and smooth your skirt, and begin to replace the items. Look people in the eye—especially men—and laugh at the situation, not at yourself. Enlist the onlookers to help you.

"Can you help me, please?" you ask in a good-natured tone. Most people will happily come to the rescue. Don't talk about how you feel or put yourself down. You are human. So you fell. So what?

You can say, "This is an unexpected way to meet people." After he has finished helping you, offer a reward, perhaps a cup of coffee. If he declines, hand him your card and say with a smile, "Well, thanks a lot," then turn and leave.

Everyone has embarrassing moments. Just turn everyone's attention away from the embarrassment of it and make it a method of meeting people. Men will respect you if you give yourself permission to be human and if you are not self-punishing when you make a mistake. Be good to yourself.

If a man does something embarrassing, like spill something, just start helping him pick it up while talking about something else. Enlist the help of bystanders. Turn everyone's attention away from the mess with talk of other things.

Be Humane. If you have an unusual breed of dog or an especially cute or beautiful dog, men will usually stop you and talk extensively about your pet. Sometimes you can meet men who are walking their dogs, too.

Walk your dog on a leash. Otherwise, you may end up meeting a man over a vicious dog fight—and meet him again in court!

Most men will deplore a woman who is irresponsible about her pet. A man will adore a woman who takes excellent care of her pet.

Pet Shops

Pet shops attract men as well as women. There is a lot of positive emotion there, and people are more attracted to each other when emotion is stirred. Plus, they interact more in an emotional setting.

Pets bring out the best in us and they are great conversation material. You can ooh and aah over a pet to a man standing nearby and he will understand perfectly.

Prepare to Be a Heroine

Take lifesaving courses from the American Red Cross, your YMCA, or other qualified organizations that offer them. The classes you take may have men for you to meet. And, besides, the life you save one day may be your next relationship!

If you never use these skills to meet men, you can certainly entertain a man by showing how mouth-to-mouth resuscition is done. And this can be a most interesting, sensuous way to kiss when you are not in an emergency.

Go On-Line

I am told that Rush Limbaugh married a woman he met on-line. I know a number of women who swear by it as a great source of relationships.

My guidelines are that you utilize good sense about personal safety when meeting men in any method, including on-line. The on-line men can lie to you and sound convincing. They may be married. They may try to get your money. Do not use this as your only method of interacting with men. You can easily sucker yourself into a mental fantasy that replaces real touch-and-experience relationships.

Coffeehouses

Gourmet coffeehouses, such as Starbucks, have replaced bars as casual hangouts for singles. Be sure you utilize the open receptive body language signals in the flirting chapter. Always sit or stand facing the main action of the room.

Gourmet coffee shops invite questions. Or, you can simply volunteer your expertise in a sincere way about a coffee blend or what to serve with it.

Have a joyous manner and a willingness to make casual small talk with everybody. You can ask a man about a drink he is trying. However, don't seem to hang on to anyone in particular.

Coffeehouses that have poetry readings or musicians are increasing in popularity also. These have a social feel to them, so making comments to someone nearby about the performance or the reading is natural.

Coffeehouses that are part of bookstores can be a great way to get to know someone better whom you have met in the bookstore. You can say, "Would you mind explaining my best use of this computer book over a cup of coffee? I am craving a decaf latte. I'll appreciate it."

Restaurant or Hotel Bars

Really posh restaurants and hotels have bars that local or traveling businessmen frequent. These bars usually have a nicer ambiance than most other bars. You can meet a girl friend—or a male friend—there for cocktails even if you have only soda on the rocks with lime.

The secret is to go twenty minutes early to see if you meet someone while waiting for your friend!

Supermarkets

Supermarkets have already become singles meeting grounds. You are doing something you have to do anyway. You are in a brightly lighted store with an upbeat atmosphere. When you see a man, you see him pretty much as he is. If you are attracted to him, you are attracted to him without the inducement of alcohol or a sexy atmosphere.

In a supermarket, you have everything in common to talk about on every shelf and every aisle. There is no shortage of conversation material. You are surrounded by it. And do stay away from the personal at first. Talk about the food or the items at hand. Keep it upbeat. Complaining is a downer.

Many supermarkets, now aware of their growing sex appeal, are adding gourmet food buffets, scrumptious desserts, and exotic coffees and teas. This way, couples who meet on aisle three can park their carts side by side while they get to know each other over cherry meringue pastry and mocha java coffee.

Lunch counters or dessert counters can also give you the opportunity to say, "Excuse me, sir. I would really like to have a serving of the chocolate fudge supreme cake, but I can't possibly eat all of it. If I buy it, will you split it with me?"

Social Interactions

Humor. If you are naturally funny, use humor . . . but use it sparingly, like seasoning. Men like humor in a woman, but they do not take her seriously for a romantic relationship if she uses it more than occasionally.

Too much humor puts you in the buddy category, or worse, comes across as silly, clownish, immature, or too insecure. More than anything else, do not use self-negating humor. Remember, you are the ultimate authority on you; therefore, if you ridicule yourself, you give your listeners permission to ridicule you.

You don't have to be funny in order to bring humor into a situation. And don't try to be funny if you are not naturally so. In other words, if you have to contrive a witty remark, don't make it! Save yourself the embarrassment of listening to it fall flat.

Instead, point out humor that is recognizable by all. You may be standing in a supermarket line and see a ridiculous tabloid headline. You can laugh quietly to yourself, turn to the man next to you, and point it out, saying, "I think that's my favorite headline yet."

Now, if he doesn't respond to you, you haven't said anything to cry about—and it is funny! Enjoy it. And probably he will find just as much humor in it as you do.

Another way to inject humor without being humorous yourself is to have an alert, positive, good nature and to laugh easily. If you overhear a man saying something funny, turn and look into his eyes and smile as if you are included in his joke. You may even chuckle quietly, too. He will probably then include you with a smile, maybe even a comment. If he only smiles, you can say something to him about his humor.

Have a contained, funny manner that he can respect, admire, enjoy, and take seriously for romance.

Double Networking. Ask a girl friend if she knows five single men. If she says yes, tell her that if she fixes you up with all five of them, you will ask each of those men to fix her up with one of his friends—thus giving her five new men from the ones she introduced to you.

Then tell her that you also know five single men (if you do) and that you will fix her up with all five of them. She, too, must ask each man you fix her up with to introduce you to one of his friends as well.

Now, do this with each of your girl friends—separately.

You are now being introduced to zillions of new men, and your girl friends are happy with the ones they are meeting.

This process can keep you dating indefinitely.

Introductions. Ask every married woman and every married man you know to introduce you to all their single male friends.

Ask like this: "I think it is time for me to meet some new men. Nothing serious. I just want to expand my circle of friends. I will appreciate it if you will introduce me to some of your male friends."

Your married friends will be much more inclined to introduce you to men they know if you make it clear you just want to meet new people. If they think you are looking for marriage, they may feel it is too big an obligation on their part and that if a serious relationship doesn't take or breaks up they could lose a friend in either you or him. Keep it lightweight.

10

Add Men and Romance with an Indirect Approach

‿‿

Not all men are the same. Many men love it when a woman approaches them, whereas some men prefer to approach a woman.

The first type of man usually has a high self-esteem because his ego does not require conquest games. The second type of man may require a challenge of hard-to-get women, just to reassure his sagging ego. That doesn't make him undesirable; it just means that if you want to meet him, you have to make him think the attraction is *his* idea—that he discovered you.

You do this by enticing him, indirectly, so that he does not even know *you* are the one creating the approach. The following indirect approaches will allow you to meet him and save his self-esteem at the same time.

THIRD PARTY

Anytime you want to meet a man, just start a conversation with someone who is standing in close proximity to him. Then, politely include him in your conversation with the other person.

INDIRECT APPROACH

Sit down next to the man you are interested in, but with your back to him. Pretend not to notice him at all. Quietly say something to other people on each side of you. Then, slowly turn around as if casually looking about you or for someone else. Do not look at him, yet. See if he says something to you first. If not, smile at someone else first and talk to that person. Gradually, include him with everyone else. Then, ask him a question.

BAD GIRL

Talk to everybody around him but him. Ignore him and force him to work for your attention. When he finally says something to you, forcing you to look at him, keep your lips slightly parted, your eyes slightly haughty. Slowly warm to him.

MEET HIM WITHOUT HIS KNOWING YOU DID IT

Notice the people he talks to. Later, start a conversation with one of those people. Do not ask directly about the man you are interested in, instead, ask a question about the person standing next to him first and then about him.

"I was told he is a lawyer," you say. "No, he's a golf pro," the person answers. Now you know what he does. Later, you can talk to someone standing next to the man you are interested in and just happen to mention your . . . uhm . . . golf lessons! Just watch everyone introduce you to him. You met him without his knowing you did it!

SOLVE HIS PROBLEM

If you are at work or at the pool or in a neighborly situation, and a man you would like to get to know complains about a problem he is having, ask him questions about it. Seem genuinely interested.

Don't come across as if you are trying to rescue—no! And never assume his problem for him. Just call the next day and pass on information to him that he can use as a possible solution. Never ask later if he did it. You are giving him an option, not butting in. If he opts to tell you, that's different.

And understand the difference between a man who is airing grievances and one who is actually seeking answers.

If he is airing grievances, he may complain about his work or his co-workers or his children or his mother. Just listen and nod but do not make suggestions. Furthermore, he needs to solve these problems himself. It stunts his personal and professional growth and creates enmity between you if you butt in.

If he is seeking answers to questions about which schools are the best, where a car dealership is located, unique restaurants, and so on, it's fine to offer information on one or two of those items.

This not only allows you to be his solution, but you can call sometime to inquire about the problem, to see how everything has worked out, or to offer him additional information. Don't be a know-it-all, though. Occasionally, even if you know the answer, just shrug so that you stay on equal footing with each other.

SETTLE FOR FRIENDSHIP

If a man you are dating is driving you wild because he is just being nice and putting you off on commitment or has given no expressions of deeper feeling, take the hint.

For your own sake, *get the message!* You stand a much, much, much better chance with him if you back off. But don't back off as a method of still trying to get him or you just continue to frustrate yourself.

If the chemistry simply isn't there for him, don't beat yourself up wondering what's wrong with you. There is nothing wrong with you. And nothing is wrong with him, either. It is okay for a man not to be turned on to you—and it has absolutely nothing to do with you.

Just because a man likes strawberry ice cream and you like chocolate doesn't mean there is anything wrong with either of you. The chemistry that turns you on to a man may be something he has, but the chemistry that turns him on to a woman may not be entirely what you have. That happens sometimes, but it doesn't make either of you wrong.

It does mean, though, that the sooner you let go, the sooner you will find someone who has the same chemistry for you that you have for him—and that is definitely good.

In order for a man to be right for you, you must be right for him in his eyes, too! No one is ever right for you who doesn't consider you right for him. And love yourself enough to vow that you can never possibly want a man who doesn't want you. That is a greater insult to yourself than he could ever give you.

If you can, rechannel your relationship with him. Settle for friendship. Meet his friends. Men tend to have friends a lot like themselves, so you may meet someone who has the chemistry that appeals to you and vice versa. This will only work if you back off from this man and stop trying to make it romantic. If you back off and suggest going places as friends without romance or obligations, later on you can ask him to get you a date with someone. More than likely, someone he knows will really, really go for you. Get him to fix you up with dates and do the same for him.

Plus, it is always nice to realize that this man is someone you can talk to and get together with occasionally when you really need a friend.

It is better to have a friendship that goes somewhere than a relationship that goes nowhere. He may never fall in love with you, but at least he will respect you . . . and so will you.

NOTICE HIS EFFORTS

We all want recognition for work well done. If you see a man working on something and comment on his work or ask questions about it, this can be a good way to endear yourself to him. You don't want to be guilty of flirting at work, since sexual harassment is a real issue today; nevertheless, you can cultivate a relationship with a man if your manner is sincere.

Notice his work and praise the quality of it. Not only that, but you may later bring the boss in to look at his work. Or, in a meeting a week later, you could bring it to the attention of the boss.

At still another time, you may very casually mention it to someone else when he is around, but move immediately to another subject so he won't be put on the spot or embarrassed and you won't seem overly impressed.

Another way to notice his efforts is to ask him to help you with the same type of work, to explain it, demonstrate it, explain it again . . .

If a man in your neighborhood is busy planting or painting or working on something outside that you can see easily without seeming nosy, you can later take a male friend or a relative by his place. Knock on his door and tell him that you brought someone by to see his work, to find out what paint he used, or such, because he did such a beautiful job.

He will likely be very pleased and very pleasantly disposed toward you after that. Introduce yourself, of course, and your male ally or relative. Ask if it is okay if your friend calls him when he begins painting or planting—that way you get his name and telephone number.

LET HIM SOLVE YOUR PROBLEM

Men like to be needed, as long as it is reasonable and not an extreme imposition. You can ask something simple, such as which school he recommends for your son who is coming to live with you. Later, you can call him to report good results from his advice.

If a man has an area of expertise, call on him for advice or help in that area. Let him know that if something else comes to mind that he thinks will be helpful in your situation, you will appreciate his calling to let you know, and give him your telephone number. Or you can send a brief postcard with that message written on it.

USE STANDARD LINES

Say "What's a nice man like you doing in a place like this?" Or look at a man and ask, "What's a nice girl like me doing in a place like this?'' You can say, "We're going to have to stop meeting like this" to someone you have never even met or to someone you encounter from time to time. And you can suggest a better place, such as the museum tea shop. Someplace unique and interesting.

Most of these lines are best said in a very comfortable atmosphere and to a man who is clearly in a genial mood.

SHATTER YOUR MOLD

Occasionally wear something different from your typical look. Wear authentic Indian moccasins and turquoise jewelry or a Hawaiian blouse. Every now and then, shatter everybody's idea of you.

It's good for them and it's good for you. It makes you stand out in a new way to some men who may have been taking you for granted or who haven't realized how interesting you are.

If you are going out for the evening, change at your office and leave in a cocktail dress. See what comments you get from men at work.

One man told me he had worked with a woman for two years and had never paid much attention to her. It was when she came to work dressed in a Santa's elf costume from a Christmas skit down the hall that he noticed her and realized how cute she was. They dated and later married.

TUNE IN

If you think you can sum up a man in a matter of minutes and decide whether or not he is anyone you want to know, you can be setting yourself up for unnecessary loneliness.

Open yourself up to experience a wide range of relationships with a wide variety of men. Decide, right now, that you are going to give just about every man a chance to prove you wrong, to prove that there is more to him than you can sum up in a matter of minutes.

You don't like for men to do that to you—to mentally wad you up and throw you away in a matter of seconds. They don't know you and it isn't fair. Tune in to what men are saying, what they are really expressing and sharing about themselves. You are going to discover a whole lot of wonderful men.

FAKE A MISTAKE

If you see a man enter an office and he is someone you would like to meet, just go into the office a few minutes later "by mistake." Pretend you are looking for another business that is listed on the directory.

Walk into his office looking for the other company. Ask questions about it. Use his telephone directory, maybe his telephone. Chat all the while, being friendly in a contained way.

By the time you get your mistake worked out, you are on good enough speaking terms to leave your card and see if he follows up.

ADVERTISE

Wouldn't it be great if you could just itemize your wants and needs in a man, like a shopping list, and submit it to be filled?

Well, why not? Sometimes you can end up with a pretty close approximation of it. Yes, advertise. Personal ads can keep your date life active and you can meet some winners.

You will definitely have to sort through some people you may never want to see again. And you should always make safety your number one priority when meeting a man or getting to know him. Gather your information and verify it.

Be honest about yourself in the ad and be as specific about yourself as you can be for greatest success. Whereas you are writing a sales piece about yourself, have a sense of modesty in your description. The ads that read "Demi Moore look-alike wants to meet . . ." can be a turnoff. I doubt if even Demi Moore would write one that way.

However, do sell yourself from the standpoint of glamour. Glamour is what men respond to most of all. You can mention that you are a glamorous redhead, or a wholesome girl-next-door type, or that you love the outdoors.

Give age range—you can fudge by five years if you have had cosmetic surgery. Give your height, body type (full-figure, petite), hair color, eye color, and complexion coloring.

As to what you are looking for in a man, be as open as possible. If you describe him right down to the centimeters, you have probably eliminated 99.9 percent of the really fascinating, really wonderful men. You want a real man you can hug, not some dream man you can't even touch, much less find.

Instead, try something like this: "Cute 5'4", 111-pound, green-eyed brunette commodity broker, 40s, is open to meeting wonderful men!" What else is there to say? It is economical, too.

Or begin it with "Wonderful men only apply to meet . . ." You get the idea.

Advertise often and respond to ten ads a week. Any respectable man magnet can fit in five minutes of phone chat or twenty minutes over coffee with two new men a day. If you are dating someone, this will not interfere at all—and it will enhance your inner strength within your existing relationships. Meet new men ongoingly until the day you are married. It is foolish to do otherwise.

If the ads you answer require letters, *never* send detailed personal letters about your life to a stranger.

S.O.S.

You will occasionally feel in the mood to do something gimmicky to meet men. Gimmicks may or may not work, but you are having fun with a little derring–do.

Let your imagination soar. Keep the guideline of harmless fun. You want anyone who gets involved to have fun, too. One gimmick can be to buy a lot of balloons, attach personal ads to them, and release them. No last name or address, just a voice mail number. This is the same principle as setting a bottle afloat in a body of water that has an S.O.S. message in it.

CELEBRATE HIS SUCCESS

If a male acquaintance gets a promotion or wins a prize or receives especially good news about something, go to him while he is in high spirits and join in, exclaiming joyfully, "Congratulations! I just heard the great news—what a winner you are! I'm not a bit surprised. You deserve it!"

Listen to him with glistening eyes and shining face while he recounts his moment of glory. Say, "Why don't we splurge on champagne and dance the night away!"

You can get away with being bolder during a moment of excitement than you can at any other time. People are so excited they feel more generous and embracing of others. So use the moment. People fall in love more during times of excitement than at any other time.

However, if he declines, ignore it and immediately press beyond it by asking more questions about his moment of success. He will enjoy recounting it to you. *He will now associate you with his happiness and his successful moment.*

Before you leave, say in your happiest tone, "That's wonderful, Bill, and I'll take a raincheck for the champagne. Call me," as if he had been the one suggesting it and you declined it—instead of the other way around. Go cheerily on your way.

STAKE HIM OUT

If there is a particular man you want to meet, study his habits. Find out his hangouts. Learn his favorite restaurants and the times he goes there. Then, wear an elegant, body-conscious dress in a vibrant color with bright gold jewelry. Wear your signature fragrance. Use your fertility curve and your magic words while utilizing your casual eye contact.

Position yourself where he can see you. Interact in a pleasant way with the server. Sit serenely for a while. Then disappear from his view. You can go to the telephone, utilizing your fertility curve as you walk. Return to his view. Disappear again. Return to his view. Then leave.

Don't return to the restaurant for three days, or until you know he is there again. Wear a different but great-looking outfit again. Sit in his view again. This time, stay only thirty minutes and leave.

The next time he is in the restaurant, try to arrive at the same time. Or you can wait where he can't see you until you see him arriving and seem to arrive at exactly the same time. Smile and casually speak to someone else first and then to him. Look terrific. You can casually chat while you both wait to be seated. If nothing develops, go to the telephone first before you are seated.

Let him get the idea that *he* discovered you. If nothing happens from his side, you can either take it that he is not available to you right now; or you can continue running into him several more times, talking to him more and more each time until he feels he knows you a bit, and see if he makes a move; or you can ask him to coffee. If nothing takes, what of it? You have had a small adventure.

Don't be a snoop, ever—and do not become obsessed with anybody! No man is worth the energy of obsession. And, frankly, obsession is an emotional high that surfaces around a control issue that is tied to your ego. Obsession is a reaction to feelings of being powerless. Becoming obsessed makes you strive for power while becoming more powerless than ever in your life!

Staking him out is more of a lightweight game to meet a particular man. You do this in order to give him the opportunity to get to know you. You also do it with a good sportsmanship attitude. If it doesn't take, don't take it personally. You don't wish to deny anyone the choice to say no. You value that choice yourself.

In conclusion, learn to violate the isolation of others in a nonthreatening manner. Learn to utilize ordinary day-to-day activities as moments to interact naturally with men.

Do so knowing that you may not only attract the man you are interacting with, but that you may also attract men who are observing your personality while you are interacting with him.

OBSERVE HIS BODY LANGUAGE

If you are at a party or in a bar, note the primary center of action. The closer a man is to the center of action, the more receptive he feels to forming relationships. The farther away from the center of action, the less receptive he feels to relating.

This, of course, depends on whether or not he had a choice of where to sit or to stand. If he had a choice when he arrived and he chose to sit or to stand removed from the action, he is less receptive.

If his body is turned away from the action of the room, he is definitely not receptive. He may only want to be around people, but not part of them. Think twice before puting on your Florence Nightingale uniform to rescue this man.

The men standing in the center of the action, fully facing everything that is going on, are the men who are there to meet people and feel receptive to forming relationships.

Once you get these many and various ways of adding romance to your daily life operating full-time, you will discover that this is just the beginning! You will thrill with self-discovery that there are an infinite number of ways to meet your lover! Go for it!

11

Add Men and Romance Through Activities

 ⌒

If you're the type of woman who is not comfortable with directly approaching a man you're interested in, here are some ways to indirectly catch his attention.

You are going to turn everyday activities into encounters with men in simple, easy ways. Utilize three different combinations each day of the following situations, and your life will be bursting at the seams with interesting encounters with men!

ACTIVITIES

Turn Off Your Television

As long as you are single, just choose one television program plus the national news or Fox News Network, some sports events, and that's it! That's all the television for you. After all, you now have places to go, people to see, things to do. Leave television for the lonely hearts and the couch potatoes. Not you, kid! You have men to meet—and that won't happen if your nights are spent watching television. Too many nights of watching television can signify depression. It can be used to avoid dealing with life. So, no more Blockbuster nights for you until you have a man to share them with!

You can't possibly meet men if all you do is stay home and watch television. Make up your mind right now that you don't care what happens on that fascinating television show, you care only about what happens in your life.

The reason you can get hooked on these shows is that the lives of the characters are so interesting. The characters have places to go, people to meet, things to do, problems to solve—and fall in love in the process.

If you tuned in to a thirty-minute show and all the characters walked into a living room, sat down, and ate junk food while watching television—and that is all they did for the entire thirty minutes—you would never watch that show again! Why not? Because it was too boring! Nothing was happening.

Let that be a lesson to you for your own life. Tune it out, turn it off, go out!

Get Involved

Your Friday newspaper usually lists weekend activities, and Sunday papers often have the upcoming week's activities. Check the lifestyle section, and check the business section for seminars. You can also check the sports section.

Don't just be a spectator who pays for a ticket at the door, be one of the people who make things happen behind the scenes. Get on an organization's committees and work diligently. However, never undertake something you cannot do or your reputation gets damaged. You will then leave the organization with enemies instead of friends if you don't do what you promise. If you fulfill the obligations you undertake, you will make a lot of new friends through the camaraderie of working together.

Then buy a ticket as a supporter of the organization and enjoy the event to the fullest! You helped create it.

You meet men at every turn when you are involved. These are men who will find you attractive because you are where the action is. And you are part of what they are doing.

Get involved in behind-the-scenes work for county fairs, rodeos, elections, holiday celebrations, festivals—anything that is going on. Visit your Chamber of Commerce and get a schedule of community events for the year.

Then begin calling the head of each event and say you are interested in volunteering time. Say that you believe in the value of the event for the community. If the first of them turns you down, go to the next group on your list and the next and the next until you find the right organization. People always need workers, especially volunteer workers. Be a doer, not just an observer.

Fascinate

If you have a special skill, put yourself forward and let people see it. This doesn't have to seem showy at all. Just make sure you do what you do best where you can be seen by appreciative male eyes.

If you like to sketch or paint, get out into the sunshine where men flock—say, in a business district at noon—and begin to sketch or paint. Men will be curious and come over to watch what you are doing, often making comments on it and talking to you. Have your personal cards with your name and number alongside you.

You can even sketch a man you want to meet. Sign the sketch, put your voice mail number on it, and, with a big smile, hand it to him before you go.

You can sketch events that are still male-dominated events and impress onlookers with your special flare.

If there are competitions for you to enter with your special talent, do so, and meet men who are competing—or fascinate male onlookers while you compete. This can include endless categories, such as weightlifting or a sailing regatta.

Whatever your special talent is, get it seen. You can do everything from practicing roping to sculpting in areas where men can see you and be fascinated by your skills.

Tone Up

Find the in spots to jog, get yourself some basic gear, and get out there! Don't set unrealistic goals that can strain your heart or your health, and, of course, always check with your doctor before beginning an exercise program. But get out there during the best hours.

Don't wear headphones or you won't meet anybody. Headphones are isolation devices that say, "Don't bother me. I'm more interested in what I am listening to than I am in meeting you."

Keep your workout clothes washed and have a minimum of three outfits you can rotate. Try jogging during the morning hours one week. Jog in the late afternoon or early evening hours the next week. Another week, try an off-time. See which hours harvest the most men and then be fairly regular in one of those times for a while. Every now and then, vary again, though, to keep meeting new men.

This is important because you are getting an idea of the types of people who jog during certain hours. This way, you can determine which group you want to identify with and which men you want to meet.

Likewise, if your doctor approves, get into a YMCA in a nice neighborhood and work out with weights. You can also join health clubs if you like. With either the Y or a health club, try all the peak periods— early morning, noon, late afternoon, evening—as well as prepeak and between-peak workout periods to see when the men are there.

Tune Up

Metropolitan areas usually have local or regional opera companies. These companies need local people as "supers," which is short for the word *supernumerary*. Don't let the big word scare you. A super is the same thing as an extra in a Hollywood movie.

An opera star may be portraying a character being put to death by villagers for a wrongdoing. While the opera star belts out her dramatic aria to the villagers, you, as a super, are one of the villagers, fully costumed and looking menacing. Some supers may sing in the chorus or they may silently be part of the background crowd onstage.

This is fun stuff. Plus, you may be joining a local surgeon, judge, or barber who enjoys being a super during the production. Again, you must be reliable. If you say you'll do it, absolutely do it. Commit your time.

You often meet famous men this way, too. Famous opera stars, opera composers, librettists, conductors . . . and who knows, maybe one of them will go for you.

Local choirs can be great fun, whether they are church choirs, school choirs, or professional choirs. Some of them specialize in pop music, others in Gregorian chants, and some in religious music. In a church choir you don't have to be a good singer, but, I repeat, you do have to be reliable and show up on time for rehearsals.

You can have more fun than you can imagine, and singing is interesting as well as social.

Dance

Dancing has been a form of courtship and socializing throughout the history of civilization.

Everything from pagan rituals to Mozart's graceful minuets in palaces to square dance hoedowns—dancing is part of every culture.

Don't be a snob about dancing. Enjoy every form of dancing you can learn. You will be amazed at how much fun different ones are.

Many country-western places have professional dancers who line up everyone on the dance floor and teach them steps to the music. You don't feel self-conscious with everyone else doing the same thing. This is known as line dancing, and a lot of men enjoy it.

For the latest hippest music, get a teenage brother, niece, or cousin to show you what's happening now in couples dancing. Modify it to your level of comfort. The main thing is to learn the in moves.

Square dancing will surprise you. I call it I.Q. dancing. It is a dance that combines your intelligence and your coordination. It is a fast-paced workout that is exhilarating; ballroom dancing ranges from sensuous tangos to graceful waltzes.

Social dancing requires men, so you get to meet men. This is something both men and women enjoy. Even when you become a wonderful dancer, try not to take over the dance floor to show off your dancing skills too often . . . but, once in a while, it won't hurt.

Play Games

What's your pleasure? Bowling? Tennis? Croquet? Blackjack? Other card games? Whatever it is that requires two or more to do, learn at least one game you can play well enough to enjoy. You might even want to compete or go to tournaments as a spectator.

The only good spectator is a knowledgeable spectator. It is the only way you can appreciate what is going on. It will also allow you to talk to men very easily. You must have an affinity that is genuine enough to attract other aficionados of the game. Knowing the game is conversation material.

Act

I have two uses for this activity. One is to use acting to become the type of woman you have the potential to become. What would you feel like, be like, act like, if you were already a powerful man magnet with men swarming around you? Act like it. You can become it.

The other use of acting is for you to take acting classes or for you to get involved in your community theater. This can be more fun than you can imagine. Even if you end up doing backstage work as a volunteer, opening night is exciting and cast parties can be incentive enough to get involved.

One of my clients told me she did this, expecting to do nothing more than hand out programs. Instead, she ended up a well-known stage actress with rave reviews.

Beautify

If you happen to like plants or gardening, you can often meet men in plant shops and at garden shows. A lot of men enjoy planting. If you are good with plants and want to enter competitions, do so; or just find out about the competitions and attend some of them.

Beautify with art, too. Attend events that focus on such male-dominated arts as carpentry, upholstering, or antique car restoration (I knew a wealthy oil man who did this as a hobby; it is a lucrative hobby, too), and visit male-loaded antique car events.

Be Adventurous

Do something daring or different from your daily life that you have never done before. And learn how to do it safely.

Write down five activities you have never done but have always been curious about learning. Make sure these are natural, passing interests of yours.

The activities on your list must include action or mental skills and cannot contain passive behavior, such as travel or seeing the Egyptian Pyramids. Travel is something just about anybody can do and doesn't require learning much in the academic or skills sense.

I'm talking about things like skydiving, parasailing, horseback riding, water skiing or snow skiing, sailing, salsa dancing, golf, chess, bridge, and so on.

Now, put a star and a number 1 next to the one that attracts you the most. Then put a star and a number 2 next to the one that attracts you second most. Do either of those two appeal to a large number of men? Are they mostly interests that you do alone, such as painting or writing, or are they mostly interests that are traditionally female-dominated, such as knitting or crocheting?

If you have a star next to them, do them anyway for your own personal fulfilment, whether or not men are involved, simply because these are natural outcries within you to fulfill a latent interest, possibly an undiscovered talent, perhaps even a new career or income supplement.

Then look through your list of curiosities to find activities that you can also use as vehicles to meet more men. Look up the *Directory of Associations* at most public libraries. Go through the directory and find as many associations—especially national or international ones—that deal with your area of interest that involve men. Telephone or write to them and find out when and where they hold their annual conventions or have trade shows.

See if there are publications you will receive if you decide to join. Find out if there are local or regional chapters you can visit—and always visit at least one meeting before deciding to join anything. Be sure you are on the group's mailing list.

Being adventurous is one of the most important steps you can make to change your life. You begin to break out of ruts you may not know you are in. You leave loneliness behind you as you thrill to new ideas, new experiences, new people, new friends, new relationships. And you will meet new types of men.

Pottery-making Shops

This is a chic new trend, even among celebrities on America's West Coast. There are pottery shops that allow you to come in and make the pottery yourself, or paint your own design on a piece of pottery before the shopkeeper puts it in the kiln for you.

To any man you see there, you can make comments about his design or ask him if he has ever done this before. If so, how he liked it. Volunteer your positive thoughts about this small adventure.

Incidentally, if it isn't very expensive, this is an excellent way to make a unique gift for a man you are dating frequently.

Be an Appreciator

Antique auctions can be interesting. And antiques can introduce you to a whole new category of men who care about quality, tradition, value, finance, and lifestyle. Check out books from your public library and learn about antiques. Take classes, browse, go to auctions. Or specialize in one area, such as nautical antiques, where you might meet elegant sailing buffs.

ORGANIZATIONS

Keep Your Mailbox Interesting

Take out your yellow pages and look up associations, clubs, organizations. Telephone every single one of them whether you know anything about it or not and have all of them put you on their mailing lists.

If they say they only do that with a membership, then just request that information be sent to you. Once you do that, you are automatically on their mailing list!

Your mailbox becomes interesting with information about all sorts of things that are going on that you never even imagined. There is always something new and interesting for you to investigate. And all these new activities lead you directly to new men. Go check out the men and see what is going on with each group.

You will get information on some weird groups as well as some excellent ones, but that is part of the fun. When you find some you like and that have the men you want to know better, join. Avoid organizations that seem too strange, but keep your mailbox interesting.

Teach Classes for Men Only

Teach classes for a YMCA, a community college, or a local continuing adult education organization such as the Learning Annex or for other independent centers. Teach fun classes for men only.

The best subject to teach is a subject you already know something about; you simply gear it for men. How about Romantic Dinners a Macho Man Can Make? What about A He-Man's Guide to Keeping House? You can do it! Come up with something different just for men and have fun meeting scads of wonderful men this way. It brings them to you—and they are your captive audience.

You can also use this opportunity to go out and meet men who are already successful in these areas, interviewing them for information for your class and using the interviews as a way to meet them!

Learn

Fun, continuing education courses such as wine tasting, ballooning and line dancing can be a gold mine of interesting, upscale men. Take action by putting class into your life.

It doesn't matter whether you finished high school or college when you take these classes. They are for fun and nobody cares. Today, continuing adult education courses that are offbeat or fun are also social in nature. Take classes for information . . . and to meet men.

Enrich Your Understanding

Did you ever wonder what it would be like to understand opera or the ballet? Did you ever wonder how people sit through a symphony without going to sleep? Have you ever been curious about why a blob of paint on a canvas is considered great art? Did you ever wonder what the characters in a Shakespearean play were saying?

There is a vast sea of self-discovery waiting for you in the world of cultural arts. I say "self-discovery" because as you learn to understand these forms of human expression you will begin to see yourself in a new and different way.

You don't have to learn all of them. But consider really learning one of them. It can make you more aware of the world you live in and can give you a finer perspective of your world.

But if you do not want to get too heavily entrenched in these areas, at least try acquiring a passing acquaintance with each one. This will introduce you to an entirely new world of people.

Call these organizations and ask if they have seminars on their subjects. Visit your public library and read about each area in the encyclopedia. Before you attend a production, go back to your library and read about that particular production. Read the history of it, the author or composer's life.

If there is music to hear, check it out or buy CDs or tapes of it, and listen to them until you familiarize yourself with it. At first, it may sound strange and ugly to you, but continue to play it softly in the background while you clean house, bathe, or sleep.

Suddenly, one day it becomes familiar and you will stand still as a poignant passage stretches across time from the heart of someone of a different century to thrill your heart today. The language of music has spoken to you.

Wave a Flag

A woman with a positive cause (not an ax to grind) can be a very attractive woman in political circles. Get involved in your political party—where you are likely to find lots of men who are active volunteers.

Working on a campaign can be a lot of fun. When you're involved with a committee, you meet more people than if you just do grunt work. There are parties, barbecues, dances, and fund-raising events galore! And you can find a committee that will fit any talent you have.

Men who are active in political parties are usually pretty savvy. They tend to be either very, very diplomatic and charming, or very, very outspoken and charismatic. It's a nice choice. Take your pick. You might even find yourself involved with a man who has a strong political future.

Dating Services

When I was single I wrote articles for a singles magazine in Dallas. One of the subjects I was asked to write about was dating services. During my research, here is what I found.

The people who run good dating services usually do their best and take their matchmaking job seriously; however, always see if a dating service is listed with the Better Business Bureau. Get references and *check the references*. See if the company has a good refund policy.

Often, the men who belong to one dating service usually belong to several, whereas women usually belong only to one.

The men in the dating services may get to know each other and compare notes with each other about the women from one dating service to the other. For example, they may tell each other who will go to bed and who won't, what she will do in bed, and how they rate her sexually.

Of course, not all men do that, but it is still something you should know happens.

Too, women over forty do not fare as well in most dating services as younger women; so you could end up spending a whole lot of money for nothing. However, if a woman over forty is fit, has taken good care of herself, she might be able to do all right.

The dating service may guarantee you a certain number of dates— but, who knows, it may have some men they can call on to fulfill the guarantee.

The most important thing to remember, though, is that while a dating service might get you a date, it cannot create chemistry between the two of you.

Still, what is wrong with having a date? I definitely think you should try every avenue open to you for meeting men, including dating services.

The best way to look at it is that you are practicing your dating skills, not expecting Mr. Right. Now, you may just meet Mr. Right, but you will have greater success if you expect a date instead of a husband.

Attend

Singles organizations and Parents Without Partners groups can bring you into contact with men who have a lot in common with you. Parents Without Partners varies from city to city. Some single moms have told me it was a godsend for them. And often it has led to marriages between couples who met there. Most of the attendees at functions like these want marriage.

Singles groups can be tricky, though. Some of these people remind me of science fiction movies where the aliens look like real people.

At first glance, they look like real singles, men and women who are there for all the right reasons of wanting to meet people, develop relationships, date, and eventually get married. But, in reality, a majority of them—the *regulars*—are really "professional singles." They *think* they are looking for someone to marry, but in truth, they are already married to the organization.

A man like this doesn't need a wife. The group fills that need. He and his wife—the group—meet mid-morning for breakfast on weekdays, for cocktails in the evening that may go through dinner. They have parties every weekend. They celebrate all the holidays together. They are there for each other if an emergency happens.

What do they need a spouse for? They don't. And so the years pass and they stay happily married to the group, while telling themselves and each other that they are looking for the right one.

Oh, the men in the group have dates and relationships with the women in the group. They seem serious at the time, but they rarely marry from the group. Too, male members and female members (and vice versa) discuss their dates quite casually with each other.

You can waste a lot of time trying to corral a regular, because he talks as if he wants to get married. Your best bet will be to meet the newcomer who really is looking to meet someone for a serious relationship.

Pray

Joining a church, synagogue, or any other religious singles group is another option open to you. In fact, it's fine to join more than one. Some churches and synagogues have active singles groups. A really good group organizes trips, informative seminars, and many activities that are not just church related but are social in nature and supportive of singles' needs.

Another plus to religious singles groups is that if you have trouble relating with people, group leaders will go out of their way to help you feel included. You can easily improve your people skills in an atmosphere that seeks to embrace you.

Again, be wary of professional singles in the religious groups, too.

One *big* word of advice. Avoid any religious group that seeks to control your life—or that gives you a bigger overdose of your sins and restrictions as a single person than it gives of encouragement and understanding.

How to Develop a Relationship

12

How to Create Dating Chemistry

Let's pretend that one winter, long ago, you caught the flu and had to stay home from work—in fact, from going anywhere—for three weeks.

You say to yourself that first night, "Well, it is awfully early, but as long as I am stuck at home, I may as well take a hot bubble bath. Then I'll slip into my snuggly robe and fuzzy slippers, pop something easy into the microwave, settle in front of the TV with my remote control, and go to bed early."

That sounds good, doesn't it? It should sound good because, after all, you're sick. The three weeks go by in the same mode—early bath, robe and slippers, microwave, TV, early bed—until you are finally back to excellent health.

After your first day back at work, you arrive home. Your telephone rings, and when you answer, a friend says, "Hello, there! It's good to have you back in the world. Let's go out tonight."

In the background, you hear your bathwater drawing up. And on the way home from work, you've stopped and picked up something for the microwave. And you definitely know what is on television tonight.

At that point you say, "Um, can we take a raincheck on it?"

All too soon, another three weeks has slipped by in this now-cozy routine. Then another and another, until it has been six months. Still another six months go by, making it a year. And then it is two years. Your life has become a routine of comfort and ease . . . and loneliness.

You are now much more comfortable being alone than going to the trouble of going out. Deep inside, though, you wish something would happen . . . that somehow you will surely meet somebody . . .

At some point, a concerned friend tactfully says, "I know the nicest man. Why don't you let me fix you up?" You agree to the date, secretly hoping that maybe this man is "the one." (When you don't give yourself choices, you have to believe that a fairy-tale "the one" will appear and rescue you.)

You go on the date and think, "Oh, no, where did he come from? He is definitely not my Mr. Right!" And you go back to your self-restricted lifestyle of having a Blockbuster night—every night. And time goes by . . . emptier. Only now, you do not think of your life as self-restricted any longer. You do not think of it as a choice anymore. You think something is wrong with you, or you think there aren't any good men.

Listen, the last time you had a date—if you thought, "Oh, no," then you r-e-a-l-l-y need to date! Because that is a sign you are losing your dating chemistry.

DATING CHEMISTRY

Dating chemistry is something *you* create. And you can measure it by taking a good look at your date life. If you do not like what you see, it is time to re-create your dating chemistry.

Being alone breeds being alone; being with same-sex friends all the time breeds being with same-sex friends all the time; and being with dates breeds being with dates.

Human beings are creatures of habit. Whatever we do a few times gradually becomes more comfortable for us to do the next time, until after a while we are very, very comfortable with that behavior. It becomes natural for us. We have then developed an affinity or chemistry with people and circumstances that are similar to that activity or behavior.

The More Men You Date, the Sooner You Can Marry

That is just how it is. The woman who would rather be on a date than watching television is the woman who will marry sooner. The woman who would rather be on a date than romping around with a bunch of women is the woman who will marry sooner.

The formula for developing dating chemistry is:

- Begin with entry-level dating.
- Begin to reaccustom yourself to be with men as often as possible by dating as many men as possible.
- Create pockets of time with men daily.
- Learn to enjoy men on many different levels.
- Play your percentages.

If you have been out of circulation for a while, your dating chemistry has dropped to a point where you may feel you don't even know how or where to begin again.

Very simply, you start where you are. Initially, you date whoever will date you! You date anybody who is sane and breathing—and breathing is more important! Okay, okay . . . I'm kidding; but you get my point.

Entry-Level Dating

Don't worry about the men you start with as long as they are decent. Basically, decent men are clean, have a steady income, and behave properly toward you. They may not be handsome, sexy, or thrilling, but as you date them, your opportunities with new men will increase.

In a career, you think nothing of starting at an "entry level" position. With dating, it is the same thing. Entry-level dating. Your body is relearning how to be comfortable with men. Your personality is relearning simple social skills with men.

Start where you are, not where you want to be. You want to date Mr. Wonderful, but if you met a Mr. Wonderful today, you could blow it because your relationship skills are so rusty from not actively dating.

As your dating chemistry grows, your dating experiences will widen and vary. You will meet new and different types of men. Just get started and the sky is the limit!

Reaccustom Yourself to Being With Men

Women who are successful with men know one important truth—that a date is just a date. A date does not have to be for a serious relationship. A date doesn't have to be anyone you would ever want to parent children with—or even introduce to your parents! A date is just a date.

Reaccustom your body to being with men. Reaccustom your personality to being with men. Reaccustom your thoughts, energy, and emotions to being with men in a replenishing way.

Pockets of Time

Women who are successful with men also know that a date does not have to be Saturday night dinner and dancing (although there certainly should be some of that, too). They know that a date can be lunch. Lunch is one hour. You can have lunch with anyone for just one hour.

A date can be a mid-afternoon coffee break. That is not more than twenty minutes of your time.

A date can be a double dip of jamocha almond fudge at Baskin-Robbins. That's, oh, thirty to forty-five minutes, maybe.

A date can be for Happy Hour after work, which is about two hours.

In other words, learn the habits of man magnets who keep their dating chemistry high: *Begin filling up little pockets of your time each day with men!*

Enjoy Many Men on Different Levels

If you are worried about whether or not a date will turn into a meaningful relationship that will turn into marriage, you are emotionally drained! Dating is then exhausting and you are worn out.

If you are summing up a man at the door with snap judgment and saying, "Well, Tom, you are a nice man, but I don't want to waste your time because I don't think we have a future together," you are cheating yourself (not to mention being a jackass).

What you are really saying is, "Sorry, Tom, you are not Mr. Right and I am such a limited human being that I cannot enjoy a cup of coffee, a movie, dinner, or conversation with any man but Mr. Right. True, he has stood me up for thirty-five years, but that lets you know what kind of a fool I am.'' Or, ''I met him once, but he dumped me, and I will not let myself enjoy anyone else until I can find a man who exactly matches his DNA.''

Have the guts to enjoy a relationship without putting a destination on it. If there is one sure sign of women and men who have ''problem relationships,'' it is that in their first meeting or date with someone, they are busy trying to figure out if this is something that could work or not as a serious relationship.

A relationship is a moment-by-moment entity. It is as free-flowing as water and stagnates if it is dammed up by evaluations, analysis, and suspicions before it has a chance to find its own level between two people.

There is a time to pinpoint the destination of a relationship, but not at the beginning. Until things have ''jelled'' between you, you do not have to know where a relationship is going. You are just going to enjoy this relationship and the next one and any other ones that follow—all at the same time—and all on their own level. That is the healthiest style of dating.

When a man asks ''destination questions'' on the first date—''Is your goal marriage?''—I urge my clients to pleasantly say, ''My goal right now is to enjoy getting to know you over this cup of coffee.'' If he pushes, say, ''Ultimately, of course. But, right now, let's take it one step at a time, if you don't mind.'' You can be a thousand times more successful in relationships if you do this. And a thousand times happier.

Dating is relationship kite flying. You enjoy the fun of the moment. And the more you do it without prophesying the future, the more exhilarating your life becomes.

How Often to Ask a Man for a Date

As long as a man is asking you out, leave the situation alone. If you have asked for the date, and if he went out with you, then it is his turn to ask for the second date. After that, you should never ask unless he has taken you on three dates.

The same is true for telephone calls. If you call a man first, then it is best if he calls you three times more than you call him.

Three to one is the best rule. It keeps you in touch, but you don't come off as pushy.

Play Your Percentages

Play your percentages. For every night you stay home alone, you must first have had three dates with men. Likewise, for every night you go out with your girl friends, you must first have had three "pockets of time" dates with men. Keep it three to one and your dating chemistry will stay balanced, sexy, magnetic, electric . . .

WHO PAYS FOR THE DATE

Dating customs vary in different parts of the country, but basically, *whoever asks for the date is the one responsible for the cost of the date*. If you ask, you pay. If he asks, he pays. It is that simple.

If a man asks you for a date and then expects you to pay your own way, he is rude. Whoever asks for the date is assuming the "host" role on the date, as surely as you or he would host a party to which a lot of people had been invited. Just because this is a party of two does not change the rules.

When a new man asks you for a date and makes it clear you are to pay your share, tell him that if you ask him for a date you will pay for it, but that if he asks you for a date you expect him to pay for it.

If he suggests you pay the next date, say "Okay" and don't call him if you can't afford to take him on a date. If you can pay for a date, and you do want to see him again, then you host the date.

Splitting the cost of a date is strictly for friends. Romance is not part of a friendship date. Let him know that.

What You Owe a Man on a Date

When a man asks you for a date, he asks you for a date, not for your commitment, not for marriage, not for sex. He asks you only for a date. A date is an activity or a period of time you spend together. That is all.

You do not owe a man anything more than what you agree to when he asks you for a date. Basically, you agree to provide pleasant companionship for the event. All obligations have been fulfilled if you are a pleasant companion.

You do not have to go to bed with him. You do not have to marry him. You do not have to love him. You do not have to do anything more than to have dinner with him if that is what he asks you to do.

Knowing that, just relax and have fun.

13

Human Inclination and Dating

According to James Bourke's fascinating PBS television program, *Connections*, inventions are built with a "planned obsolescence" that caters to "human inclination." What is human inclination?

Human inclination is a level of interest in something that changes through a cycle of saturation, which works like this:

CYCLE OF SATURATION

- Interest in something.
- Involvement with it.
- Tiring of it.
- Rejecting it.
- Seeking something else.

It is this very cycle of saturation that causes the natural ending to most relationships. I believe that most relationships end from boredom, not from any real problems. I further believe that when problems begin, it is because of boredom.

Have you ever seen a child acting up in church? The child is bored. Being bad is more interesting than being bored. Even being punished for being bad is more interesting than being bored.

The cycle of saturation is to blame when a man begins cheating or spending time pursuing other interests. It is not that he intends to be a bad person, he has simply completed the cycle of saturation with his primary relationship. The cycle of saturation is human inclination. How many times have you said, "Rex is nice. He is just too nice"—and turned away from a relationship with a good man who did nothing worse than bore you.

Sometimes, our choices of mates have less to do with deep psychological patterns than they have to do with our individual thresholds of boredom.

Germaine left charming Allen for rowdy, bawdy Ralph. "It's not unfinished business," she said. "The loud, boisterous ways of Ralph are more interesting to me than mild-mannered Allen. He is so boring."

Compatible Cycles

Couples who have similar cycles of saturation are in sync with each other. Each automatically introduces a new interest before the tiring phase has appeared or just as it has begun. They cycle together.

Look back on a relationship that you felt ended due to something lacking in you. You can probably see that you and he had a different saturation cycle in a relationship.

Ways to Prevent It

The cycle of saturation happens most frequently if you become too predictable, if you commit too soon by giving up your other dating relationships when he has not asked you to—and sometimes even if he *has* asked you to. Women have been taught to be too pleasing, too restrictive in expressing our need for variety. Release the fascination of your personality while dating and don't be afraid to show your knowledge, your curiosity, and your playfulness. Think of ways to keep the relationship interesting—for yourself, *not* for him—and he will likely find it more interesting also.

YOUR DATING PERSONALITY

There are three elements that should be evident in your personality with a man that help move you from dating into a more serious relationship.

1. Emotional variety.
2. Limiting your impulses to please him.
3. Stability and fun.

Emotional Variety

A kaleidoscope fascinates with its variety and combinations of colors and unique patterns. Your emotional patterns in a relationship are colors that also create a fascinating kaleidoscope that make you different from any other woman he will ever know.

Cherish your emotions. They are the building blocks of your personality. Your relationship exists in your emotions. They are the guideposts that let you know if you are in a healthy relationship or not. Your emotions are your expression of life. Hold them dear.

All the emotions you have make up a wonderful part of you. Learning to see your feelings as an acceptable, lovable part of you will give you strength of personality and charisma.

Learning that it is okay to express them effectively gives you power in relationships.

Spread your emotions in a beautiful array around yourself like the proud peacock's fan.

Celebrate your emotional variety: joy, anger, fear, affection, jealousy. Feel all your feelings and express them appropriately without letting your emotions run amuck. You don't owe a man an apology for your emotions or how you express them.

How a Man Feels About Your Emotions. Actually, a man likes to feel he has to "deal with" a woman's emotional variety. That is what makes a relationship have life, energy, triumph, and momentum.

When a man is busy harmonizing with a woman's emotional nature, he cares about her very much. He finds her interesting and absorbing. Her emotional variety adds dimension to his life.

If a man ever criticizes you for expressing your emotions, *do not apologize for your feelings.* Defend yourself and he will respect you more than if you were to grovel with an apology.

Say, "I won't apologize for being human. I like the way I am."

A man responds emotionally to your emotions. The emotions you generate in him are the fruit a man returns for time after time.

Limiting Your Impulses to Please Him

Now, you are an adorable lady who wants to be gracious. I know that. At the same time, I want to teach you to protect yourself from letting this trait be misused.

Women who have the most difficult time in relationships are those women who try too hard to please a man. The same is true for women who try to displease a man.

You want to have an overall lovable quality to your personality, but without trying to please. **Nothing can sell you out faster than selling out yourself to try to please a man**.

No matter what a man says, he will be disappointed if you try to please him. Please yourself and you will please him all the more.

Simply "Be." In our busy world of do, do, do, we sometimes apply the same "do" ethic to our need to be loved. Yes, there are certain do-this and do-that behaviors that can generate an interest in us from men.

But in learning how to be loved, there is only so much that you can *do* and then you must simply *be*.

*Be*ing requires a willingness to merely be present among people and to *do* nothing. Just being can bring a tremendous sense of relief and power. For the first time, you may be aware of how exhausting it used to be when you were with men before.

Men sense the calm and ease of just being that you now have. You are not acting shy or standoffish or self-conscious or rude. You are fully present. Men will respond to that strength of self-acceptance in you.

Do What You Normally Do. Part of just being is to do whatever you would normally do if you were alone in the same situation, to behave the way you would behave if he were not around. If he wants to include himself, fine. And you will respond in your true emotional state about it.

Say what you would say if he were not around, and say what you think, no matter what he thinks about it, in a simple, easy, nonoffensive way. This behavior allows you to be yourself. Being yourself means flowing with your natural energies to express yourself. If you are lively, talkative, witty, or intense, and direct, or soft-spoken and demure, flow with your natural energies no matter what they are.

By flowing with your natural energies, you are being you. This is the uniqueness of your style of doing things. Your flow of energy is what is meant by personality.

As long as you direct your natural flow of energies through a positive channel, cherish the wonderfulness of you. It is this positive and natural flow of your unique energies that a man falls in love with.

Be Willing to Make Dating Mistakes. It is okay to make mistakes and to say the wrong thing on a date. It is okay to make an absolute fool of yourself occasionally. Everybody has a cache of embarrassing dating moments they can't stand to remember.

Mistakes are the common denominator that makes us human.

You only learn how to be with men by dating and being with men. That means you are going to make mistakes. Say to yourself that you are willing to make mistakes with men and on dates in order to attain your overall relationship goals. That's the only way you learn!

Be Playful. Tease him about his cowlick. If you feel like bursting into song, do it! Just be you. Sometimes the funny little things you would do just with your family are the cutest expressions of you.

Be Sassy. In a fun tone, say, "No, I won't do that" to something he asks you to do. Sassiness is best done with a smile on your face or a mock sense of disdain.

Scold Him. Don't criticize, but do scold. Make him go back to the rest room and put the toilet seat down. Send him back to scuff mud from his shoes. Straighten his tie with a "Tsk, tsk" that it was not straight in the first place.

Compliment Him. Tell him how nice he looks occasionally. When he is dressed up to take you out, light up and say, "How nice you look!" or "What a great-looking tie." Don't overdo this, but let him know in small ways how you appreciate him.

Be Wise About Your Territory. Familiarity breeds attraction in many cases, so why have your girl friends around your man?

Don't feel overly confident in your man's loyalty or feel sorry for your friend because she is lonely and unloved. You can't imagine the numbers of friends who have walked away with the mates of their beautiful girl friends.

Gabrielle is a stunning beauty who had the devotion of her man. She felt sorry for Margot, a plain woman she worked with who had not had a date in years. Gabrielle invited Margot to visit and to go out with her and her mate.

Stan complained in the beginning that he didn't like dragging Margot along as a charity case. Gabrielle felt so sorry for her, though, that she continued including her. That is, until several months later, when Stan left Gabrielle for Margot.

Be a Date with Standards. Set standards as to how a man can relate to you and you will be more successful with men. For example, *never* let a man come over to see you late at night when he has been somewhere else without you during the evening. Never!

Be a Date, Not a Servant. Do not clean a man's apartment, wash his car, do his laundry, tend his plants, walk his dog, type his reports, cook his meals, do his homework, weed his garden, rake his leaves, organize his garage sales, or host his parties for him. If you do, you are setting yourself up to be used big time!

A man will not like you one bit more for doing all this for him. He may like that you do it, but he won't like *you* more for doing it. He may even like you less. He may feel you have a hidden agenda to obligate him to you.

If he asks you to help him rake his leaves and if you want to do it as an outing, have him help you do something of equal effort *first*. Never do his housework or laundry for him, ever.

Be a Date, Not an Adviser. It will be very, very tempting . . . especially when you can clearly see the solution to the problem he is complaining about . . . but resist telling him anyway.

When a man is complaining about his job, he doesn't really want your advice, although he may seem to want it. He is just mulling it over out loud. He is sharing with you his feelings of confusion, but, believe me, he wants to make up his own mind on the matter.

This isn't male pride or chauvinism. He just wants to make up his own mind about his own life, just as you do. He may even ask what you think, but you should say only, "I am sure you will come to the best decision on the matter."

If you advise him and he doesn't take your advice—and at some point, he won't—you will feel frustrated. He will feel frustrated, also like a failure, somewhat resentful, and over time, stubbornly rebellious.

You are his date, not his guidance counselor. Do not advise him.

Be a Date, Not a Banker. Never loan him money. If you are not married to a man, forget about helping him out financially. This is the fastest way for you to lose him.

He will realize he can use you—and use you he will! He will also avoid you if he is due to pay you back or to give you a return on money you supposedly gave him as an investment. He will begin to lie, wheedle, and do everything but come through for you financially.

If you want to support a man, that is fine, but keep it clean. Consider a onetime, flat amount that is a gift he does not have to return to you.

Or see an attorney and work out a way to pay a man a salary for contracted jobs he performs for you or an "allowance" that is a flat amount given at regular intervals. No advances. No other money favors.

I urge you not to give him money at all for any reason and to tell him that you simply do not loan money, period. No apology and no discussion.

Don't Be a Victim. Don't complain about how he treats you, because it positions you as the victim. Don't accuse him of not caring for you, because that does the same thing. Stay away from negative talk.

And don't confess your faults. Jo Beth used to tell a man on the first date all her faults because she thought she was being fair and upfront with them.

The men she dated thought she was nuts. It is expected that you put your best foot forward when you begin a relationship with anyone, knowing that the rest will take care of itself.

Emo Talks. Men overdose on too much "relationship talk," too much let's-solve-our-problems, emotional-cleansing talk (emo talk). A certain amount of it is necessary for healthy relating, but gauge yourself by listening to at least one of his discussions about his work or his favorite sport—and really, *really* listen. And be sure the two of you talk about fun, light topics as well.

Deep, soulful talks may make you feel closer, but they don't guarantee he will end up treating you any better. One of my clients found a man who had taken seminars on how to communicate with women. Apparently, the advice was good, because she was thrilled at the rapport they developed. They had in-depth emo talks by the hour. However, he called abruptly one day, ended the relationship, and went to Europe with another woman.

He had learned good information, but he used it to lead women on and to enjoy their falling for him. It made him a better communicator, not a better person.

Learn to Say No. Ginger thought it was polite to be agreeable; therefore, no matter how she really felt about something, she would always agree with people. Unfortunately, she found she was quite lonely and never sought as a leader, never popular with men or women.

Realize that you can disagree and still be agreeable.

Make a list right now of ten activities you don't like. Now, pretend a man you like has suggested doing one of these items on your list—bowling, for example.

Say out loud, "No thanks."

Pretend he persists.

Out loud, hear yourself say, "You can go bowling if you want to, but I don't like that game."

Pretend he gets indignant: "Oh, come on, you never want to do anything I like."

Right now say, "Don't ask me again. Otherwise, I am going home."

You will be respected as having character if you learn to say no to friends, associates, and men. Women who say yes all the time make themselves puppets. They engage in sexual conduct that degrades them or they take drugs because their men do. They are afraid they will lose a man if they disagree with him. In fact, you will lose him, anyway, if you agree with him all the time.

Sharon went to bed with a man when she wasn't ready only because he said he would never see her again if she didn't. The relationship did not last. If a relationship cannot develop through respect, rest assured, the relationship will not develop *without* that respect.

Be Audacious. If a man makes an observation of you or says something slightly critical in exasperation—such as "You are so stubborn!"—have a few audacious quips handy and use one.

"Yes, I am!"

"I like it!"

"Oh, good!"

"I was hoping you would say that!"

"Why, thank you!"

"I promise never to change."

"Well, at least I'm not as bad as you are!"

"Now that I know you don't like it, I'll do it every chance I get." (Said with an impish smile. This one may prevent his criticizing you further.)

Bounce Him Out. Get out of any relationship where *real* criticism exists. You don't need a man who belittles or ridicules you. A man who is mentally abusive will not change. Accept that and move on.

If you can't disarm him effectively with audaciousness or hold your own by distracting him with a few darts thrown his way, then you are in for a severe mental and emotional beating throughout the relationship that will only harm you.

No Explanations. If a man tries to put you on the defensive by asking questions you do not want to answer, answer him with a nice question, such as "Why do you ask?" or just say, "I will not be questioned.'' You do not have to be confrontational in your manner—but you do not have to be subservient, either.

Stability and Fun

To develop a relationship beyond casual dating, a good man responds best if he sees you as both stable and fun.

Stable You. The stable side of you is a woman who is responsible. You project a stable image if your home is basically orderly, clean, and comforting, if it smells nice and you smell nice. (Yes, I know this may mean tossing everything under the bed when he calls and says he wants to stop by and see you.)

You are seen as stable when you have the class to go home from a date at a decent hour, instead of dragging in when the sun comes up. Going home while you are having fun together is the hardest time to do it, but do it anyway. Keep him coming back for more by leaving just slightly before the more runs out.

At the beginning of a date, tell him you have to be in by midnight. Men actually like it when you don't leave it up to them to end the date. They will also like you more if you are not keeping them up until daybreak when they have to work the next day.

Sure, there are special times when that happens, but they should really be rare, special, and very romantic.

Fun You. The fun side of you incorporates ''enjoyment'' into typical, daily life. For instance, put him to work for *you* when he arrives. Have him put out the dog. If something is going on in the news, ask him to read a particular article about it in the paper out loud to you while you are putting the finishing touches on your makeup or hair or adding your accessories.

When he comes over during the day or for a casual evening, have him help you peel shrimp or chop onions or shell peas for cooking. Incorporating him into your life in a natural way adds enjoyment.

And it also adds fun by bringing out the child in both of you. Have him take you kite flying. Have a picnic in the park and swing or seesaw.

Stable and Fun. If you only seem to want fun and games, a man will find it difficult to take you seriously as a marriage partner because you would come off as unstable. If you are too serious, a man will think twice about making you a marriage partner because you would seem too boring . . . not fun enough.

Learn to balance stability and fun.

14

Love Gifts

You will never go wrong if you always buy a gift for a man within the context of the relationship. You will rarely suffer the humiliation of having gone overboard with a fabulous gift when he has forgotten you.

GIFT CONTEXT #1 —
NEWLY DATING ONE MONTH

It can be very tempting in the tingly high excitement of new love to let your heart open your pocketbook—but don't do it!

Even if you are seeing each other every day, even if you are already sexually involved with each other, and even if you have both declared love for each other, stick with gifts that are appropriate to the length of time you have been dating.

Appropriate gifts for one month of dating would be one of the following and range from $1 to $25:

- A cute or funny card.
- A bottle of his favorite liquor.

- A small plant.
- A hardbound book.

If you write anything on a card, keep it very light, cute, and teasing.

If he surprises you with a greater gift, do not feel bad about yours and do not apologize for it—ever. You have acted appropriately.

The underlying message of a gift for one month of dating is simply: "You are a nice person," which is proper and *effective* for the time you have been involved.

GIFT CONTEXT #2—
DATING THREE TO SIX MONTHS

Let's say you are more madly in love with him than ever at this point and you are sexually involved.

If you are seeing each other only once a week—or less—*or if* you don't know for sure that your relationship is exclusive—*or if* for any reason you have ever felt insecure in the relationship—the only appropriate gifts are still those in context #1.

However, if you are seeing each other virtually every day—to the point that it would be unlikely for anyone else to be in the picture—plus, mutual declarations of love have been made—plus, you feel secure in the relationship—then you can give gifts that have a little more meaning.

Still, keep a $50 limit on the gift itself—and do make it a gift that brings a smile rather than overwhelms.

- Personalized writing paper.
- A handsome pencil/pen set (not Mont Blanc or Cartier).
- A handsome sweater or cardigan.
- A fairly exotic plant (if he will take care of it).
- Tickets to a single event (*not* season tickets).
- A tie (not Hermes).
- Massage oils.
- A name-brand fragrance.

- A paperweight.
- A creative gift.

It is very important during this time period that your creative gifts do not give the impression that you knocked yourself out to impress him with your creativity.

Do not monogram anything other than writing paper. Monograms are too personal. Remember that at this stage the relationship can feel permanent, but it isn't yet!

GIFT CONTEXT #3 — LIVING TOGETHER

Gifts in this category depend on whether you are living together for mutual convenience or as a precursor to marriage.

If marriage is the objective, then go gift shopping together—perhaps at a mall. This is vitally important! It prevents relationship problems from his having forgotten your birthday or your anniversary or Valentine's Day.

Just a few days before the event, say, "Sweetheart, our anniversary is next week. When you get off work tomorrow, we are having a sandwich at the mall after we spend an hour in separate stores buying each other a gift."

Agree on a cost per gift, which, at this stage of your relationship, can be from $100 on up, if that is affordable. Check your watches and agree to meet each other an hour later with wrapped gifts and cards.

Then have a second gift that you select together as an investment in the relationship, such as joint stock, joint insurance, joint real estate.

Incidentally, getting a marriage license or setting a marriage date can be a mutual gift! The holiday itself can generate a specialness in a holiday wedding.

Use holiday gift giving as a way to nudge the relationship forward to swift consummation in legal vows. The longer it goes on as is, the less likely it will end in marriage—so move on it this holiday!

The underlying message of your gifts for each other during this relationship and time context should be a mutual "I do!" of commitment and love.

15

How to Evaluate Dating Relationships

~~

I have helped many women understand the realities of their relationships with the following information. I even received a thank-you from a psychotherapist in New York who, for three years, had been trying to help a woman understand her relationship. He said that going through my bona fide relationship cases with her made her instantly aware for herself.

DO YOU HAVE A BONA FIDE RELATIONSHIP?

Usually when a woman complains about a relationship it is because she does not have *a bona fide* relationship with the man in question in the first place.

A bona fide relationship is one in which both people have the same goals for the relationship. You will know if a man has the same goals for the relationship if:

- He has the same or similar expectations as you.
- He has the same level of interest in you as you do in him.

Let's consider the following four cases:

Case 1

Mr. X is in your town on business once a month and likes to have someone to go out with. He thinks you are fun and enjoys going out with you when he is in town, but he has other people to go out with also.

Let's say that you have an active social life already; however, you find Mr. X very entertaining. You like going out with him when he is in town as long as you have nothing else to do.

Do you have a bona fide relationship? Yes! You and Mr. X have the same goals for the relationship—an occasional good time together.

Case 2

On the other hand, let's say that you do not have an active social life. You are a workaholic career woman and you intend to stay that way. However, you do enjoy Mr. X and usually need the break from work when he happens to be in town.

Do you have a bona fide relationship? Yes! Again, you both have the same goals for the relationship, which is an occasional good time.

Case 3

This time let's pretend that you have a fairly active social life, but no other man can compare to Mr. X in your eyes. You find yourself counting the days until you see him again. You hate it each time he leaves.

You find yourself wondering if he sees anyone else and the thought eats at you. You have begun to press him for information about his personal life, and he is evasive.

You have made suggestions that one of you move to the other's city, maybe even live together. He says that would be a problem for him at this time, maybe later. You tease about the two of you getting married and he changes the subject.

You telephone him a lot; however, he usually calls only to let you know when he will be in town.

Do you have a bona fide relationship? No. You have different goals, as shown by the different expectations and levels of interest you each have.

As sometimes happens, in Case 3 you have created a relationship in your mind that does not exist, and it becomes a time-stealing torturer.

Case 4

Let's further say that you have told Mr. X you love him and he says he loves you, too. He reassures you there is no one else. He says he wants the two of you to be together, maybe even to get married later on—but still, he makes no move to change the situation and gives plausible-sounding excuses to delay changing the situation. He may call daily or only occasionally, but it is mostly to give his itinerary and to make plans for when he is there. He may talk for a while, but usually he mentions meetings or how busy he is when he closes the conversation.

Do you have a bona fide relationship? No. Clearly, Mr. X does not want to hurt your feelings, but he does not want more from the relationship. Believe behavior, not words. He is lying—not to hurt you, but to keep you in the picture for his goals.

What are his goals with you? Very likely, his goals fall into one of the following categories:

- He likes you quite a bit, but he has not determined whether you are what he wants.

- He likes you and knows you are not what he wants, but he hasn't found anyone better suited for him, yet.

- He has no interest in ever having a relationship with anyone that requires serious commitment. He can happily continue the convenience of the relationship he has with you at its current level.

None of this indicates an inadequacy in you, although you may feel it is due to something lacking in you. It isn't. It means only that you do not have a bona fide relationship.

The longer it goes on as is, the less likely it will ever be anything more to Mr. X. It is important for you to find out from his behavior, not his words, whether or not this is going to be a bona fide relationship at the level you want it to be.

If you and your Mr. X have been seeing each other monthly for as much as eight months and your goals fit case 3 or 4, then you should begin finding out as quickly as possible if you and Mr. X have the same goals of a serious relationship or marriage.

In order for a man to be right for you, you also have to be right for him—and his opinion, too. The only way to be right for a man is to have the same goals for the same relationship and to have the same level of interest in each other, which makes it a bona fide relationship. Anything other than a bona fide relationship is not a relationship but a fantasy.

Can you make it into a bona fide relationship? The best you can do is to:

- Find out his goals by evaluating his behavior. That is all. You cannot force someone to feel something he does not feel.

- Accept the relationship on his terms indefinitely, without holding on to false hope.

Examine yourself to see if you can change your view of the relationship and downgrade your expectations of it to the goal level he has, which is casual and occasional enjoyment of each other.

If you can do this, and if you can begin caring more about other men and have less interest and less attachment in Mr. X, then you can have a bona fide relationship because you will have the same goals he has, such as those that are in the category of case 1 or 2.

End the false relationship if your goals are different from his, but only if it is causing you pain. Put him on the back burner of your life and open yourself up to experience other men without comparing them to Mr. X.

If you have serious goals, actively enjoy many relationships until you meet men who have serious relationship goals with you, too (and you eventually will). Go ahead and get married. Then simply drop a brief card to Mr. X asking him not to call (and mean it) because you have gotten married.

A bona fide relationship, however, is not immune to flaws. How well you understand flaws in a relationship can make or break the future of the relationship.

Compatible Flaws

You have seen "Ken and Barbie" couples that have everything in common. They are both good looking. They both ski. They both love the symphony. They look good together . . . the list goes on and on. Yet, for all their compatible interests, their flaws make them incompatible . . . and the relationship ends.

You have seen other couples that make you think, "How on earth did those two ever get together? They are so different from each other. They have so little in common . . ." and yet they celebrate anniversaries year after year after year together, still in love.

Why? Because the couple has compatible flaws. I have found that in long-lasting relationships, it isn't so much what a couple has in common that makes them compatible in the relationship. It is that they have compatible flaws.

Having compatible flaws does not mean that a man's flaws won't bother you. They will. Any man you are ever involved with will have flaws that will drive you straight up the wall—and your flaws will do the same to him.

The difference between incompatible and compatible flaws is that compatible flaws may put a terrible strain on a relationship from time to time, may upset you outrageously at times, even hurt you or him at times—but *compatible flaws don't damage the relationship*. Incompatible flaws are those that damage the relationship, sometimes in major traumas or sometimes in slow, small, but irreparable ways.

For example, Joe and Sybil divorced because of Joe's drinking. Joe held a good job and kept his bills paid. Sybil did not like that he always stopped for an hour after work to have a drink and that when they both came home from work, he smelled like beer. Football Sundays were beer and pretzel afternoons. Plus, she was embarrassed when they went out with friends and he got drunk. She begged him time and again to seek treatment, but he shrugged it off. Unable to handle this situation anymore, Sybil broke up with Joe.

Joe later married Maureen, who did not view his drinking as a problem. She knew it was not best for him, but it did not interfere with his earning effectiveness and it did not interfere with their marriage.

Joe was a cheerful man, sober or not. Although she didn't drink much, Maureen met him after work when he had his beer. His Sunday afternoons were times when she got away for herself. If he got drunk at parties, she felt he had the right to make his own choices about it and just made sure he did not drive home.

So who was right—Sybil or Maureen? Both Sybil and Maureen were right. Joe's level of drinking was an incompatible flaw for Sybil. It was a compatible flaw for Maureen.

The One Impossible Flaw

There is only one flaw that makes a man an impossible mate and that is if he has any priority ahead of his relationship with you.

If his priorities are right, you can make it no matter what his flaws are. If his priorities are not right—by that I mean if he puts violence, job, parents, children, friends, personal interests, addictions, playing around, money, religious views, or anything else ahead of his relationship with you—then you don't stand a chance together, I don't care how great a guy he is otherwise, or how flawless he seems. If his priorities are in the right place—that is, if his relationship with you is number one over everything else—and he treats you as number one, then you can make it together as long as his flaws are compatible with yours.

Three to One Counts Most

A man can have several flaws as long as each flaw is countered by at least three assets.

He is controlling, but he is also always on your side, a great lover, and affectionate, all of which fulfill and satisfy you beyond belief.

Counting three to one, he has more assets than flaws. If his main flaw does not dominate his assets, this man deserves your time and attention.

If he has three flaws to every one asset, that is another story. If he is controlling, unsupporting, and cold, then his great lover quality will not save him, if that is his only redeeming trait.

Flaw Degree

If he is controlling, how controlling is he? Does this flaw immobilize your own goals in life? Does it flare up frequently, but not daily? Does his effort to control you ease up when you call him on it or when you refuse to go along? Or is it that you cannot do anything because he negatively counters every decision, ever comment you make? Does he manipulate you in subtle ways that you realize only afterward? How often does it happen?

Yes, a flaw may surface from time to time, inconsequentially, but does it dominate the relationship? Do your flaws dominate the relationship? Do you both value your relationship more than anything else? One person cannot make a relationship. It takes two to make it happen, to make a relationship mix.

Relationship Mix

The unique way in which two people combine their flaws and assets results in a relationship. A relationship is the blending of your emotional patterns with the emotional patterns of a man.

The way these blend together or do not blend together creates the relationship mix between people. The relationship mix either works, doesn't work, or works for a while.

Even with more assets than flaws, how does it stack up against your relationship mix? Are his flaws compatible with your flaws?

Sometimes a flaw is the energy of a relationship. It can be the stimulus for interaction. The flaw may stimulate emotional drama and actually create the magnetism of attraction between two people.

What if you have the same flaw as the man you like? This is not a doomed combination, necessarily. It depends on the relationship mix between you.

Controlling Flaw, Example 1: If your undesirable trait is that you are also controlling, you can be sure sparks are going to fly between you—and often—over every decision from the simplest, such as what to order for dinner, to more important career and family decisions. Still, the controlling flaw may be the magnetic energy between you.

I know a couple, married seven years now, with this dynamic control issue. Both find the constant sparring both aggravating and exhilarating.

In fact, when an observer offered a solution, they stopped mid-spar, both stared at the man, and said, almost in unison, "This is the way we dialogue," and then went back to sparring over whether or not to check their child's carseat as luggage at the airport.

"Dialogue?" Yes, that was the very same word both used, which is why it has stayed with me. Their control traits not only create an ongoing battle, but have become almost a dance of interaction that is important to the chemistry of attraction in their unique relationship mix.

Without the control issue, they would both feel bored. Their relationship would be as flat as champagne left uncorked for a week. And that's just fine. It works for them. No one controls the other. The control flaw is a compatible flaw in this relationship mix.

Controlling Flaw, Example 2: If you have the control trait and cannot stand for anyone to argue with you, then, no matter how much your soul cries out for the other nourishing qualities you adore in this man, you would probably not consider the ongoing sparring to be "dialogue."

You would consider it a challenge to your judgment. You would not consider it an emotional dance but a constant state of frustration and aggravation. You would be miserable and seek escape. And that's fine, too. The control flaw is an incompatible flaw in this relationship mix.

Controlling Flaw, Example 3: Your flaw may be that you are too agreeable and somewhat indecisive. You may be fairly laid-back and not interested in controlling anything or anyone. You like to be around men with dynamism and direction.

Your friends may complain that a man is controlling you. But, frankly, you prefer having someone else in charge. Besides, he sticks up for you, helps you get things done you have been putting off. The control flaw is a compatible flaw in this relationship mix.

You cannot simply sum up a man by listing his flaws and then dispose of him unless he exhibits the one impossible flaw of having other priorities. You must weigh a man's flaws in proportion with his assets and then evaluate *your* flaws and assets in the unique relationship mix of the combination.

How Important Are Assets?

So now that his control trait is not an issue for you, how do his assets mix with yours? Are his assets desirable to you? Are his assets and flaws both compatible or incompatible with yours? Examine yourself to see how much you value his assets.

Women who complain ''. . . after all I did for him . . .'' are realizing that what they considered assets were not what their men considered assets. You can be holding pure gold in your hands, but it if isn't gold to you, it won't do you any good. The biggest reason assets are valued or not valued has to do with a person's love tolerance level.

Love Tolerance Levels

Love tolerance has everything to do with whether or not you get your emotional needs met in a relationship. This is where the belief system comes back into play—and it can wreak havoc on you until you become aware of it.

We all have a tolerance level of the amount of love we allow ourselves to receive from someone. The love tolerance level is based on our inner love scripts.

If the man you love believes he does not deserve a woman who loves only him or who would be faithful, then his belief system will go to work on that premise, screening out a woman who loves him with more devotion and loyalty than his love script allows.

You will know you have exceeded his love tolerance because he will begin to distance himself or to blame you for something unrelated to love.

A man can change his love tolerance level, but he must be at a point in his life where he is seeking to change it. You cannot change a man's love script. He will not let you. That is why you must realize that if you have been good to him and he rejects you, it was not that you failed, it was that his inner love script did not include the level of love you gave. You exceeded his love tolerance.

What created his love tolerance? The way he interpreted events in his life led him to make choices or decisions about what the events meant about him.

For example, his mother might have died when he was very young and he might have interpreted the event to mean that he had been bad and then made the decision that if he loved someone, she would die.

He might have had a very efficient mother who did her best to take good care of him, provide everything he needed to thrive. He might have decided he was the most wonderful person in the world who deserved a loving female who would be his emotional support system while he achieved greatness. If a woman is so involved in her own career that she is not there for him, she falls short of his love tolerance needs.

He might have observed his parents' constant quarreling and decided love meant fighting. If you do not fight with him, he may think this is not love.

When you talk to a man, find out about his relationships with his parents when he was a child. Which one was he closer to? How did they make him feel about himself?

What are the positive and negative qualities of his mother? Does he have unresolved ego needs caused by his parents (almost all of us do)? What are they?

What was the relationship like between his parents? Has he had relationships with women that were similar? Which parent's role was he most like in the relationship? Did his former lover or ex-wife have traits similar to those of one of his parents? Most likely, she had traits similar to those of the parent toward whom he has unresolved ego needs.

But relationships do not just deal with his love tolerance level. They also deal with yours. Let's look at your love tolerance in the next chapter.

16

Are You Living Someone Else's Love Script?

$\backsim$

What if you went into a dark theater every day to watch the rehearsal of a live play. Day after day, for several years, you hear the same dialogue over and over and over until you know it by heart.

One day, the lead female does not show up. You know her part so well that you automatically get up onstage and begin reciting her lines.

This really did happen to you. As you grew up, you heard your mother say phrases over and over. You saw the way she moved through her day and the way she handled relationships. You were the understudy for your mother's role. You know it all by heart.

And, unless you were encouraged to be you—unless you were given permission by either your mother or your father to say different lines— then very likely, as a young woman, you began living someone else's script for your life.

ROLE-MODEL SCRIPT

Your lifestyle may be different from your mother's, but is your relationship life like your mother's? Do you have the same problems in relationships even though the circumstances are different? If so, you are living your mother's love script, not your own.

You may have learned how to relate to men by watching how your mother related to men. Mom might have been the only role model you had.

You may unknowingly be mimicking your mother's role in relationships. You may feel that you don't have permission to outshine Mom, permission to live your own script.

Recently, I read that a famous movie star said her daughter, also an actress, had "inherited" her mother's bad luck with men. When someone suggested that her daughter's luck might improve, the movie star said it wasn't likely.

I am sure she intended her remark to be light and funny, but unintentionally, it is a remark that does not give her daughter permission to be more successful with men than Mom.

"Don't outshine Mom," it says. "Mom was unlucky in love so I have to be unlucky. Can't compete with Mom and win." You haven't felt permission to live your own script.

ROLE-ASSIGNED SCRIPT

You may be living a role you felt was assigned to you within the dynamics of your family. What was your role? Caretaker? Outcast? Perfect child?

You may be continuing the unhappy role in your relationships with men. You may be the caretaker with men. You may select men that reinforce your outcast image with your family. You may be unhappily paired with a man who fits your "perfect child" image with your family.

You may find yourself feeling a lack of permission to be anything other than the role that was assigned to you.

Is your relationship life the way you want it? If not, you may be living someone else's script for your relationship life.

RIVALRY SCRIPT

Has there always been a lot of animosity between your mother and you? Nothing you did was ever good enough and you were always wrong. Were you closer to your father? Did you feel your mother interfered with your relationship with your father?

If so, it may be that your mother felt threatened by your birth, fearing that you would be more loved by your father than she was. This is more common than you know. If your mother had trouble with her own mother or had to compete with sisters for attention, this can be especially true.

Such feelings are a double bind for your mother, who loves you and at the same time feels threatened by you.

It is a double bind for you, too. You love your mother and yet you also feel impaired by her. You may get the message that you cannot compete with some other woman (a psychological surrogate for Mom) for a man you want and win. This may lead to recycling the role in love triangles or involvement with married men.

HIDDEN SCRIPTS

Sometimes a daughter lives her mother's hidden script of frustrated desire. If your mother disliked marriage but stayed in it because she felt dependent on her husband, she may have inwardly yearned to be single and earning an independent income.

Even though you may really want to be married, you may find yourself living your mother's desired life of staying single and being independent. You picked up on her desire and have acted it out for her.

REWRITE YOUR LOVE SCRIPT

Most mothers do not intentionally send the messages you receive, so let's not give them a bad rap. *Moms can be seriously flawed and still wonderful, too.* Their messages were an automatic response to something they feared in their own environment. Too, they may have been unhappily living out their own mothers' scripts for them!

Whatever the cause, you are you. And you are responsible for getting your needs met, now. Your mother isn't. You can stop living someone else's script for your life by writing your own love script.

Rewriting your love script is easier than you think. All it takes is creating:

- New role models.
- New familiarity.
- Script therapy.
- An increase in your love tolerance.

New Role Models

Role models provide scripts for their roles. You may have had poor role models for women or you may have ventured into territory where you had no role model at all.

Choose a woman who has a relationship life you admire. Just study her. Dress like her. Imitate her behavior. Then choose another woman. Do the same thing. Then another.

Through them, you are trying on new ways of being, just like trying on new clothes, to see which ones give you the best results and make you happiest. Happiness with results means you are striking a chord of something that is really you.

Your choice of role models will be an intuitive part of your own potential or you would not have been attracted to it.

New Familiarity

Were you ever the new girl in school or new to a neighborhood or job? At first, it felt strange because it was unfamiliar. A year later, you knew your way around. It became familiar to you.

You now make different choices of behavior—choices that may feel strange to you at first because you are not used to them. But, as you practice being the new you, with new behavior, over and over, it will become familiar and comfortable.

Script Therapy

When you find yourself feeling down or insecure or unhappy, ask yourself what "messages" or lines from your old script are triggering these feelings. Using a chart similar to the one below, write them down under "Lie." Then cross out the sentence with a heavy line and rewrite the opposite statement under "Truth."

LIE	TRUTH
~~I am worthless.~~	I am valuable.
~~I am wrong.~~	I am right.
~~It's all my fault.~~	I am responsible only for me.
~~No one likes me.~~	People like me.
~~I can't win.~~	I am a winner!
~~I am stupid.~~	I am intelligent. I am bright.
~~I am a loser.~~	I am a winner.
~~I'll never be anything.~~	I shall be what I choose to be.
~~I am guilty.~~	I am responsible only for me.
~~I am bad.~~	I am good.
~~I am fat.~~	I love my body.
~~I am ugly.~~	I choose to express beauty.
~~I am unwanted.~~	I want me. I love me.
~~I have no one.~~	I can count on myself. I won't let me down. (Even if I am afraid I will, I won't.)
~~I'll never have what I want.~~	I can have what I want. It's up to me.
~~I don't exist.~~	I exist. I am.
~~I am lazy.~~	I am a doer. I am filled with enthusiasm.
~~I am not important.~~	I am important or I would not exist.
~~I make mistakes.~~	Yes! And I am still lovable!

When you write the truth side, eliminate the word *not*. For example, instead of writing "I am not stupid," which is negative, write instead "I am intelligent," which is positive.

Also, write all statements "in the now"—as if they already exist. If you write "I will be thin" that keeps your truth in the future. By continuing to state it only in the present, it pulls your truth into existence "in the now."

A study of illiterate adults who wanted to read revealed that their inner scripts determined whether or not they succeeded in learning to read. They wanted to read, but inside they thought "I can't read." And, sure enough, they didn't learn how to read. Their success rate was dismally low.

Then they were told to arrive for class, to receive their books, to sit down at their desks, and to say "I can read," out loud, twenty-one times in a row.

Only after saying these words could they open their books and begin the lesson. The success rate was astonishing! These illiterate adults of all ages became competent, skilled readers. Some even went on to receive academic degrees—all because they rewrote their inner scripts.

WHY CRITICISM IS A LIE

When people say vicious things to you they speak out of their own limitations, their own shortcomings. They say lies to hurt you. They are trying to control you, to limit you to their scope of life, rather than to see you outdistance them. Their lies express fears they believe about themselves that they project onto you. And often, they say the opposite of what is true about you. Therefore, destructive words are actually lies.

WHY COMPLIMENTS ARE TRUE

Interestingly enough, compliments are true! That is because compliments require some degree of objective analysis. Even flattery requires a modicum of truth. The intent of the flatterer may be in question, but a modicum of truth is there, nevertheless.

Keep a list of compliments everyone gives you. Write down the compliment, who said it, and date it. Read them to yourself often.

YOU HAVE TO CHOOSE

If you have believed the lies, then at some point you have *chosen* to believe the lies because you believed someone else was more of an authority on you than you. But that is impossible. They are not you. And they do not choose for you. You do.

The beautiful thing is that you can rechoose. You can create your own truth of being all that you want to be. The illiterate adults chose to rechoose. They chose the truth about themselves they wanted.

Choose to believe good about yourself, not bad. You are the sum total of your successes, not your failures. Seek only what is right about you, never what is wrong. Ask only what you did right. You are good. Focus on that.

Somewhere inside you, you know you are good. You know you are really on your side—as you were born to be. You have taken better care of that little baby you than you realize—and now that you understand it, you will take even better care of your little baby you.

Once you know the truth, you can never fully go back to believing the lies. And now, you do know the truth. *You are wonderful.*

INCREASE YOUR LOVE TOLERANCE

By rewriting your love script, you will also increase your love tolerance. You see, we all have a tolerance level of love that is based on our inner scripts. If your inner script reads that you are worthless, fat, and ugly, and that no one can ever love you, then your belief system will go to work on that premise, screening out anyone who loves you more than your script allows.

You will know your love tolerance by the types of relationships you have. Plus, if a man loves you more than your script tolerates, you will begin to "distance" him by starting fights, acting bored, being irritable, or criticizing him. You may have affairs or flirt in front of him or get drunk and embarrass him or make a scene or stand him up or disappear. All because his love for you exceeds your love tolerance level.

If you don't believe you are wonderful, you cannot accept men who think you are wonderful and you end up emotionally starving yourself by sabotaging relationships. That is because you do not want you. You transfer that feeling about yourself onto each man who is willing to love you—that he is not what you want.

You will also know this is your love script and love tolerance level when it seems that the men you do want don't want you. This is especially true if you longingly pine in torment for a man you cannot have.

You don't have to do that anymore. You can enlarge your love tolerance by changing your love script and your belief system.

When you convince yourself that you are wonderful by insisting on it with your magic words, you will find you can accept men who think you are wonderful and who treat you as if you are wonderful.

17

Former Lovers, Ex-Wives

Former lovers, ex-wives, and children are part of relationship terrain today, so you need to know the lay of the land and have a good clear road map for navigating your way around in it. Otherwise, you can get so lost in a maze of previous relationship traps that you feel like Dr. Livingstone, who disappeared many years ago in the wilds of Africa!

FORMER LOVERS

A former lover who writes letters, hangs around, calls, shows up, and makes a general pest of herself is obsessed with your man. She is not emotionally finished with him. And she hangs on to the idea that she can rekindle his interest in her.

You have to figure out if he is enjoying the game, even though he complains about her, or if he really wants to be rid of her.

If she is just a pest and he wants to be rid of her after a breakup, he will not answer his telephone. If he is tricked into taking a telephone call from her, he will make a transparent excuse for not calling back, tell her he will call back and not do so, or tell her not to call anymore.

If she comes around, he will have a reason for not seeing her and

will leave immediately. He may even tell her he is involved with someone else, hoping that will sink in.

If she is vengeful, and if he really wants to be rid of her, you will
know. He will have his telephone numbers changed. He may move. If
necessary, he will have a restraining order placed on her by the court.
If she violates it, he will have her put in jail.

If he enjoys the game, he will take calls, read letters from her, and
so on, even though he complains about it and tells you he wants to be
rid of her. If that is the case, do not hang around waiting for him to
come to his senses. He consents to her game. It is a depraved courtship.
Move on.

PLEASANT EX–WIVES

If an ex-wife has married again or has her life together and doesn't
call except to say what time she will be by to pick up the kids, consider
yourself in dreamland. This is a woman you can like.

But while you can like her, don't make the mistake of thinking you
and she can be friends. Your intimate relationship with your mate has
to be your top priority and should never be watered down by being his
ex-wife's buddy.

Her views of him could affect your view of him. You could end up
having the same relationship with him just because you anticipate the
same problems, based on what she has said. And what she tells you
may be out of her own hidden agenda of not wanting to see him happier
with someone else.

An ex-wife who acts as if she is a friend can be deadly in her effect
on the children, because her influence on the children is so subtle.
Whereas she may want her children to have a relationship with their
father, she does not want the children to have a better relationship with
their father than with her. If she thinks that might happen, she will
ridicule his life and his choices, and criticize what he does with them.

More than anything else, the "nice" wife does not want her children
to end up liking you too much. She feels competitive for her children's
affections and does not want them associating you as a type of mommy
replacement since you are with Daddy.

It is a rare ex-wife who isn't just slightly curious and maybe slightly jealous of you as her replacement. Ego may cause her to compare you with herself. She may not be as nice about you behind your back as she seems to be to your face.

She may also be nice as a way of disarming you to gather information from you. To play it safe, watch your conversation with her and with the children, who will certainly pass on to her anything that is said. Be sweetly vague if she or the children ask the following questions:

- "Are you planning to get married?" This is a loaded question. Disarm anyone who asks by saying "We're just friends," even if you and your mate have discussed getting married.
- "How serious are you two?" Same answer as above.
- "How long will you be here?" Say "I don't know."
- "What kind of plans have you made for the holidays?" You say, "I don't know, yet," even if you do. Or you say, "Oh, the holidays! They seem to creep up on everybody, don't they? What are you and the children doing for the holidays?"
- "How do you feel about Sam [your new man, her ex-husband]?" Say "We are just friends" or "He is very good with Jake and Annie [their children]." You have deflected the question away from you and Sam to Sam and her children.
- "How often do your children see their father?" This is another loaded question. Say "As often as possible." Say this even if your children's father never visits your children.

If You Have Children

Even if you loathe your children's father, do not reveal how you feel about him—and don't discuss his lack of visits with her. If you do, it will come back to haunt you later.

She will certainly mention what you have told her about your ex-husband to her own children, and they will talk about it to your children, maybe cruelly.

If you have children, she is concerned that Sam may end up being more of a father to them than to their children. On any questions, give vague replies and change the subject by telling her about a movie you and Sam took the children to see. Tell it scene by scene if you have to in order to avoid further personal conversation.

Or, instead of answering her, glance at your wristwatch and say, "I'd love to talk longer, but I have to make a telephone call right now. It was great having the children with us. I think they are telling the baby-sitter good-bye now. Nice to see you." And go!

She may truly like you or she may only *seem* truly to like you. It makes no difference. Your behavior is the same. If she isn't a trouble-maker, be nice, be friendly, but be smart—*protect your relationship from ex-wife influence*.

PROBLEM EX–WIVES

A troublesome ex-wife will pull out all the stops—guilt, blame, and shame. And she knows all his hot buttons to do it, too.

His duty, his obligation, his responsibility. Blame, accusation, and more criticism. And, furthermore, according to her, it's all your fault. He is putting you before his very own flesh and blood—the innocent children who were in his life before you were! Shame, shame, and more shame.

Don't put up with problem ex-wives. Any ex-wife who still calls for advice or comes over is infringing and has no rights to fairness or to anything else—that is why she is an ex. *Ex* means "no more rights." *Ex* means "no more anything in this man's life." This is all the more true if there are no children.

Psychologically Still Married

Have your mate and his ex-wife slept together occasionally since they divorced? Do they spend Christmas together with the children? Do they have lengthy talks on the telephone several times a week? Do they meet for coffee or dinner when he brings the children back from visi-tation or vice versa? If so, they are still married psychologically and are only technically divorced. They have not consummated their di-vorce. Their conversations are peppered with "My ex." "My ex did this . . ." or "My ex did that . . ." This is no different from saying "My wife did this . . ." or "My wife did that . . ."

The word *my* is a personal pronoun that shows possession. The possessive use of the pronoun *my* denotes a lingering connection. All divorced people occasionally use this expression, especially if they are around other people who are talking about their ex's that way, but when it is used a lot, it can represent a continuing status of possessive connection.

When a man's divorce has been emotionally consummated, he usually says, "Pat did this . . ." or "Josh's mother did that . . ." or "The woman I was married to at the time did so and so . . ."

In order to be emotionally free, people must divorce not only on paper, but also divorce each other's possessions, divorce each other in their behavior toward each other, and divorce each other in their speech references to each other.

Mixed-Message Fantasies

Children can get a mixed message about their parents' relationship from hearing this type of talk. They may then live in a perpetual fantasy of getting their parents back together and consider it their responsibility to make it happen. That's a big, tough job for a little child to feel saddled with—and all because of Mom's and Dad's mixed messages.

And you? Oh, you get caught in the middle of this with your own fantasy, too, if you are not careful. How can you be careful? Simple. Don't try to be fair to an ex-wife who is floating around in the periphery of your relationship with your man. If you do, she can make turkey stuffing out of you.

You will be giving her far too much advantage with him because you will be acting as if you are in second place, as if she is really in first place because she was there first and was once legally married to him and you are not. You will be acting as if she has rights. You will be acting as if you are only a substitute for her. Nothing could put you in a weaker position.

Fairness to her is not your job. That is the job of his lawyer and her lawyer. You will come up short if you try to win the Nobel Peace Prize in your man's former marriage. Make it clear to your man that once you and a man have verbally agreed to have a sexually exclusive relationship, you owe your allegiance to each other over anyone else. You must clearly proclaim the superiority of your position in his life.

You must be territorial about your rights and what he owes you over her, or you will lose him.

No Trophies for Second Place

If you are second to his children, then you are second to his former wife. This means that you—in his present life—are in second place to his past, which means you don't have a future. Don't accept second place to a man's past.

If you have to, make him decide if he intends to live in the past or in the present. He may still be his children's father, but he is not still in the situation he was in when he was living with them. Remind him of the mixed messages everyone gets if this is not clarified.

DISCUSSING AN EX–WIFE OR FORMER LOVER

When you discuss any ex-wife or former lover, do not accuse him of still caring for her. And don't remind him of how badly she treated him. That gives her too much credit, too much power.

Instead, when you speak of her, do so as if you consider her pitiful, pathetic, a loser, powerless, inferior. Remind your man that since the divorce is final there is no reason for contact between her and him for advice or help of any kind.

18

Children—His, Yours

IF HE HAS CHILDREN

Paula got involved with Carl, then got caught in the cross fire by agreeing to stay overnight with her new man's children in his home while he went on a business trip. Carl called later to tell Paula that under no circumstances could his ex-wife take any of the children's toys or clothes he kept for them at his house.

Sure enough, his ex-wife came by the next day to pick up the children. The children gathered their favorite toys and his ex-wife started to pack their clothes. Paula stepped in and refused to let her do so. The children started crying. The ex-wife insisted she had paid for their clothes and an all-out uproar ensued.

Do you see what this man did? He used Paula to do his dirty work for him. His children heard Paula refuse to let them have their toys, not their Dad. Even though Paula told the children of their dad's instructions, they will always remember that Paula was the one who didn't let them have the toys. They will always remember *her* as the one who was fussing with *their mommy*.

He avoided being the bad guy in front of his children and avoided the scene with his ex-wife. In the end, he dumped Paula, saying he didn't think his kids liked her! Later that year, he married a woman who kept her relationship with him separate from the children and his ex-wife.

Jarod and his daughter moved in with Angela, whom he planned to marry. In a short time, it became clear that his little girl loved Angela very much. Jarod, however, slowly began to withdraw. Sex tapered off until he finally told her he wanted to sleep on the sofa so he could work at his computer late at night without disturbing her. Before the year ended, he and his daughter moved out.

Jarod only *thought* he wanted to find a mother for his little girl, until he began to feel that he had lost his singular position with his daughter. Jealous and unwilling to admit it, he became increasingly morose about it, increasingly resentful. He could only reclaim his "top dog" status with his daughter by moving out.

Betty and Jeff lived together for six months and decided to marry. His teenage daughter, who lived with them, announced one morning that she was pregnant and she didn't know who the father was.

Jeff became terribly upset but said he would pay for an abortion. The teenager refused and this started a fight that continued for about three weeks, with Betty jumping in to take his daughter's part.

Jeff gave his daughter an ultimatum: get an abortion or get out without help from him. His daughter packed her bags and left.

Betty left, too. She said she could never marry a man who could treat someone that way. He begged her not to go, but she cut off all contact with him.

That was four years ago. Betty has not married. Jeff has. After the baby was born, he and his daughter settled their differences. He is sending her to college and paying for baby-sitting for his grandson.

It was okay for Betty to defend the girl and to comfort her, but it was foolish for her to end her relationship with a man who treated her well because of his initial reaction to his daughter. People change after they have had time to think things through. The daughter has no contact with Betty. She is close to her dad, though. So, it worked out for everyone but Betty.

* * *

Craig was a widower with three grown, unmarried children. He was also close to his aging mother. Darlene was divorced, with a small son, and knew she wanted to marry Craig. After they started dating, she took his twenty-three-year-old daughter on shopping trips. She took baked goods to his mother. Darlene told Craig how much her son adored him. In all, she made herself a part of the family.

When Craig did not call Darlene for weeks, she called his daughter, who stammered an excuse and got off the telephone. Darlene took more baked goods to his mother, who had seen Craig three times that week but did not know his whereabouts.

Craig had gotten married. He married a woman who had only said hello to his daughter on the occasions she was with Craig. She had never met his mother. She had two children of her own that Craig had only greeted a few times.

Do not try to ingratiate yourself to a man's children or family. He will resent it. The children will be suspicious of it. They feel that you are using them to get their father or son.

Gloria wasted three years on Ted. He swore he loved her and wanted to marry her. However, he delayed because of problems with his grown children. Just wait, he promised, until he helped his son work out his college problems, which took a whole year. Then his daughter needed a place to live, just for a while.

He had the impossible flaw of having priorities over Gloria. He gave his daughter priority to his house over Gloria.

A man can use his children as an excuse to hedge or vacillate. This is another way to avoid commitment. Although he can make himself sound angelic, idyllic, noble, and honorable that he is thinking of his children and being such a good father, the reality is that he is hiding behind his children and using them as an excuse not to commit to you, not to make you number one.

He is not ready for an adult relationship, and you are letting yourself in for meddling by children and for second-place status with him. That is a no-win situation.

Remember:

- Do not be a baby-sitter for his children.
- Do not try to be a second mom.

- Don't get involved in problems with his children.
- Do not ingratiate yourself to his family.
- Don't let him use his children as an excuse.

IF YOU HAVE CHILDREN

If you are a single parent, you may tend to make peers of your children. You talk to them as if they are your best friends. You confide about adult problems to them. You may unwittingly move your child from best friend into spouse position and not be consciously aware you are doing it.

I am reluctant even to say the words, but you need to know that the term used for giving a child spouse-position priority is *emotional incest.* I know you would never intend this—never—and that is why I am telling you about it.

The result of emotional incest from spouse-position priority treatment is that if you one day fall in love and get married, your child will feel every bit as betrayed as a wife does when she finds her husband has left her for another woman! Your child will feel cheated on, emotionally lied to, and filled with depression and anger.

It is not something you would ever intend, but it is something that can happen almost without your realizing it.

Do Not Involve Your Children

You may also feel that it is important that your children by a previous marriage be involved with your new husband-to-be. This is not true. All too often, children end up in one of several unfortunate situations with new spouses.

- **Competing with your new mate.** Feeling threatened, they test you to see who means more to you. They create a power play by causing trouble between you and your mate and making it seem as if it is the mate's fault.

- **Becoming a pawn of your ex-husband.** Your child, hearing complaints from his or her natural father about your new man, may "act out" the natural father's contempt toward your mate. Remember, your child will likely feel loyalty to his or her father and consider the new man in your life as something of an enemy.

Also, your child may unwittingly become a tale bearer as his or her natural father asks questions about you, about your new mate, and about your relationship with each other.

- **Being violated sexually, physically, or emotionally.** Yes, your child could be victimized by a man you are dating. A man you could never believe would do such a thing! *Don't trust any man with your children.* I mean this more than I can say.

   Your new man is not a daddy replacement. There are things you can never know about someone, I don't care how long you have lived with him. Be positive that your man would never molest your child by never affording the opportunity.

Susan Smith, the young woman in South Carolina who murdered her two sons, had been sexually exploited by her stepfather, who is a leading citizen in her community. He looks and seems nice, respectable, trustworthy, yet he seduced her when she was barely in her teens and continued having sex with her even after she was married! You cannot tell a man's morality by the position he holds or the way he looks or the philosophy he espouses.

Even if you think this man would never do something like that, why put the opportunity in front of him? This is your child! You are responsible for his or her sexual safety in this situation. Your new mate should not be your baby-sitter, ever! That is usually when molesting takes place. And most children don't tell, even when encouraged.

And don't overlook the numbers of deaths each year of children who were beaten to death by stepfathers who were baby-sitting the children while their mothers were at work. Why risk it?

WHETHER THE CHILDREN ARE HIS OR YOURS

Children can know they are loved and also know they do not have spouse-position priority in your life. Once a child is made aware of a parent's relationship priorities, the child will actually feel more secure. A child knows that she or he is a child and that it is wrong to give a child dominion and spouse-position priority. Children actually feel more secure knowing the parameters.

A child may feel that, because she or he was born before the relationship between you and your new mate was established, she or he is entitled to priority over your marriage partner.

Not true. One day your child will be an adult and will fall in love and want to marry. If you do not like the person your child wants to marry, do you think your child is going to give you priority over his or her choice of a mate? Not likely. Your child probably will not (and should not) give you spouse-position priority in his or her adult life. It is unhealthy for either parent or child to have precedence over either's spouse.

Children need to understand the No Trespassing signs in their parents' lives as much as they should understand that your love for them is unconditional.

19

Four Types of Relationship Fights

Understand that *physical violence is never an acceptable fight*. When I use the word *fight* I am referring to verbal arguments, highly inflamed disagreement, contradicting, maybe shouting.

Some fights are healthy to your relationship and some fights are not. All fights are mirrors of deeper dynamics of your relationship and deserve close evaluation and respect for what they are telling you. Remember, anger is your friend. Anger is a warning light emotion. It tells you that standards have been lowered or violated to the point that you are letting yourself be hurt.

HEALTHY FIGHTS

Healthy fights are those that bring you closer together afterward. These include fights of ventilation, clarification, and adjustment.

Ventilation Fights

Couples sometimes let small hurt feelings accumulate. This can be okay if the offense is small, accidental, or rare, but if it happens enough or over a period of time, these repressed feelings can cause deeper problems if they aren't addressed.

Logical discussions are preferred, of course, if they resolve the problem. Sometimes, though, logic doesn't make a dent for either of you. Fortunately, a good fight can actually solve the problem. These fights unplug emotions that could harm your relationship if they remain unexpressed.

Swallowing anger is absolutely futile and potentially damaging when his inconsiderate behavior runs roughshod over you. Your feeling of anger is telling you that it is your responsibility—now—to teach him how to treat you. He will never learn it any other way. And it is your job to teach him.

It is his job to teach you how to treat him, too. Between the two of you, there may be periods of unplugging the cork on accumulated hurt feelings and anger. These fights ventilate the relationship of emotional and behavioral debris. After such fights, the relationship works better. The two of you are closer. Sometimes there is actual improved behavior by one or both of you.

Clarification Fights

Sometimes, no change is necessary . . . just a clearing of the air. A better understanding of each other. Much like the cut of surgery that hurts but is necessary to work on the damaged inner organ, these fights can actually be healing in some ways. Once healed, the body of your relationship functions in greater health. You are closer.

Adjustment Fights

Healthy fights can include those that occur when one or both of you have had expectations that conflict with reality. He or you may have had expectations about the other or expectations of your relationship or expectations about a situation that simply are not going to be met.

Repeated disappointment and frustration with unmet expectations finally builds to the point that a fight erupts—a fight that adjusts each of your expectations with reality. It is a fight that bursts the bubble of expectation, but it also replaces it with something better—realistic substance. The fight adjusts your understanding into something you can both live with better. You both feel closer.

WARNING FIGHTS

Too many fights may be a sign of boredom, that it is time for you and your mate to discover new areas of interest together. Too many fights may be a sign that your relationship is already emotionally dead in some areas, so that fighting becomes the only method the two of you can use to generate enough emotional stimulation to prove to yourselves that you both care.

At least when you are fighting—although you hate the fighting—you are both pulling out a strong level of emotion, an energy that proves there is still life in your relationship somewhere!

This is a red flag to develop new areas of your relationship, not to take each other for granted.

FIGHTS OF SEXUAL REPRESSION

Sex, too, may be stimulated by the emotional energy of fighting and making up later. This may be especially true if your daily relationship doesn't generate enough romantic juice to turn you both on with desire for each other; or if you only have sex after enough time has passed that it has built up inside you to the point that it is a physical release.

Sometimes, it is that very buildup of overdue hormonal release that can trigger big-time fights—perhaps from the resentment of having to wait so long for sex or from repressed sexual fulfillment.

Don't feel bad about hormonal buildup sex. That happens from time to time in practically all long-lasting marriages due to many outside stresses. However, when a couple becomes dependent on fights (*real* fights, not sexual play-acting) as the only way to fuel sexual interest between them, it is not healthy fighting and not healthy sex.

Too many fights indicate that the energy of the relationship has been reduced to one dimension. Marriage requires a multidimensional relationship with more peace than conflict.

FIGHTS OF DYING LOVE

Fights of dying love do not bring either of you closer. Fights of dying love slowly disconnect you from each other. The fights are petty and frequent. There is no simple ventilation, no clarification, no adjusting to a reality that makes you feel closer to each other. The fights do not result in a deeper closeness. The fights result in deeper, lasting hurt. The fights do not ventilate anger. The fights increase the anger and frustration.

Most of the time, in a dying relationship, when you are fighting, you are fighting your own denial of the truth and so is he. You and he do not want to face the truth that one or both of you have feelings that are dying. But anger does not let you live in denial. Anger continues to push and push, harder and harder, increasing the fights until there can be no more denial.

Anger increases instead of diminishing in dying relationships. There will be an almost constant discord. There will be increasing rage in fights to create the energy that will catapult one or both of you over the final hurdle of denial and into the truth.

The truth then is a realization and acceptance that there can be no resolution of relationship goals between you. The fights, which include nonsolution and you-end-it fights, have served to disconnect each of you from the lie of your relationship, like disconnecting the life support machine from someone who is technically dead already.

When you are fully disconnected from each other, the suffering is over. Dying love fights actually help you disconnect from each other. They help you get out of denial and into dealing with the truth. These fights eventually set you free to find new love.

Nonsolution Fights

Nonsolution fights may sound much like ventilation fights. In reality, one or both of you is simply "dumping" petty irritations that have absolutely nothing to do with the relationship.

Oh, one of you may be blaming the other for the problem, but the fight has nothing to do with what the other person did. The aggressor is operating in a low threshold of irritation and can be set off by the merest thing. It could be something as insignificant as the expression on your face.

It could be over something insignificant that you or he bought. It could be absolutely anything that sets either of you off. The telling traits of a nonsolution fight are that it is petty, nothing is ever good enough or pleases enough to keep anger at bay, it is unexpected by one of you, it accelerates, it hurts, it inflames more anger—and there is no solution. When the fight ends, you do not feel that anything has really been resolved.

You-End-It Fights

One person doesn't want to accept responsibility for the end of the relationship and so, through fights, is pushing the other to the breaking point so that the other person eventually will break it off. The person who pushes the fights is actually the one who forces the other person to end it.

HEALTHY ANGER IS YOUR FRIEND

Consider healthy anger to be your friend, for it is. Anger provides you with energy—adrenaline—to give you the extra power you may need to force a situation into the open, to face it, and to deal with it. Your healthy anger is trying to protect you from harm, to warn you that you are allowing someone to overstep boundaries in your life.

Healthy anger rises if he runs over you, jokes about your shortcomings to friends, forgets your birthday or anniversary, is rude or inconsiderate of your time, money, beliefs, or feelings, and doesn't heed your warning or takes you for granted. Introduce him to your friend anger with all flags flying.

If you imprison anger, it will tunnel a way out—possibly damaging the walls that hold it in with illness, disease, or petty spitefulness to others that can alienate you more.

And be sure you do not hurt yourself in the process of acting out your anger to him. Do not hit the wall, and hurt your hand. Do not kick the table, and injure your foot. This is unsafe behavior of misdirected anger toward you. Yell at *him*. Scream at him. Get it all out to him. He is the one who deserves your anger, not you. Do not be angry with yourself for being angry! Respect it. Let it flow in words toward the man threatening your happiness.

UNHEALTHY ANGER

Do not hit him in any way. Hitting him can endanger you, also. In many cases of spousal abuse, murder of a spouse, or injury to a lover, a woman struck her mate first, thinking he would never hit her back. In some cases, he never had hit her before. A man may react automatically, and if he does, there can be no going back on your part. Shred a pillow, if you must. Destroy easily replaceable objects if you must. Do *not* strike him.

There is another reason not to hit him. You do not want violence and rage to become the emotional kingpin of your relationship energy. If you do, it will become very sick and it will eventually fail.

Physical abuse is not a way of proving how much two people care for each other. It is a symptom of how sick the relationship has become.

Unhealthy anger is rage over a minor infraction that is far out of proportion to the situation. Unhealthy anger is punitive in nature. It belittles, scorns, destroys, humiliates, and is cruel.

Physical abuse is a no-win relationship. You want a win-win relationship. Do not hit and do not tolerate being hit. It is not love.

Anger is a survival emotion. Your anger is fighting to save you from eventually hurting yourself more through the delusion of denial so that you can pursue real fulfillment for yourself.

ANGER RESOLUTION

You want ways to express the buildup of anger that will not be destructive to your relationship. The following steps are useful to that end.

Listen to the Anger

Let your partner vent his anger in full while you sit and listen. Listen, intently, for the source of violation he feels caused the anger. Do not interrupt or argue. Listen, listen, listen.

His anger will have three stages. The energy of it will accelerate in the beginning as he talks about it. It will eventually reach a peak and slowly decline. You will know when he has finished because the energy will wind down until he is simply repeating a few things over and not taking it anywhere.

Question the Anger

When you determine he is close to finishing, ask him, "What do you want me to do about it?" or "How can I help you?" Again, listen very closely to what he is saying. Is it fair? Is there justified pain? Can you do it in all fairness to both of you? Do not argue.

Resolve the Anger

This is where you and your mate begin negotiating trade-offs. Try to keep this from refueling the anger. Keep your mind on resolution and keep his mind on it, too. He has had his turn to express his anger, now it is time to defuse it, entirely.

Can you have your turn with anger? Yes, but if you are really trying to solve a problem it is best if you do not do it at this time. Show him your solution grit this time.

20

How to Know If a Relationship Is in Trouble

IF HE CHEATED ON YOU

If you are the one who has been cheated on, don't just blame the woman. It took two of them. He was a willing participant—and your man owed you more loyalty than she did if you have both agreed to monogamy.

You may consider this to be the most devastating experience of your life. Handling this problem will call for the greatest self-control you will ever have to face—if you want to emerge the winner.

If He Does Not Know You Know

Yes, I know that you will want to confront him, to show him that you are no dummy, that he was not able to fool you! Your pride and your rage will urge you to tell him you know.

Your inner dialogue will sound something like this: "He can't get away with cheating on me, because I'm leaving!! How stupid does he think I am? How could he do this? How could he hurt me this way?

How did I fail? What did I do wrong? Why wasn't I enough for him? What does she have that I don't? Is she better than me in bed? He must not love me. Maybe he never loved me. Maybe he loves her.''

Your inner dialogue is a mix of fresh pain, raw anger, fear, distress, grief, love, and hate. And, yes, if you dump it all on him, it is okay with me. He deserves it.

But what if you could postpone telling him you know about it until you have time to decide what you really want to do. During the frenzy of emotion, you may think you know what you want to do, but you don't. Your feelings will change many times before you really know what you want.

Wouldn't you really rather outfox him? Sure you would. And you have three choices to base your action on.

1. You still want him.

2. You want him, but you really cannot live with him after this.

3. You do not want him anymore.

You Still Want Him. If you still want him, your best bet is not to let him know you know about it. If you tell him you know about it, you may force the relationship past the point of no return. *You are not denying the infidelity in your own mind, you are just choosing not to give it more significance at the moment.*

Do not tell friends about it. If friends try to tell you about the infidelity, refuse to listen. Remember, you still want him.

Seek counseling from a psychologist who will respect your decision not to tell him that you know. Or enter a support group where you can talk over your feelings with others who are dealing with a similar situation.

Protect yourself sexually. Tell him you are concerned about a possible vaginal infection or something that will seem to justify the use of a condom.

Grieve. Tell him you received sad news about a friend (you did). Be very good to yourself—good nutrition, vitamins, exercise, as much rest as you can get under the circumstances.

Above all, refuse to obsess about her. Do not follow her or watch them or call her place. Refuse. You want to rise above this, not let it drag you down and destroy you.

Gradually begin new interests outside of your relationship with him. Take classes. But most of all, take it easy on your heart.

If You Cannot Continue With Him. Even though you feel you cannot continue with him, do not tell him you know about his affair. If you are living with him, do not leave for at least four months. This is very important.

Every change you make in your life creates stress. When you found out he was cheating, the stress on you became pretty great instantly. I know that staying with him under the circumstances is, in itself, highly stressful, but if you leave during this time, you will compound the stress.

Get a Plan. If you are going to leave him, you need a financial plan if you have been living together. Begin setting up your life change in secret, just as he set up his affair in secret. Do not tell friends or ask if they know. They will tell him. See a psychologist for moral support.

Lease an apartment and spend a little time in it each day to accustom yourself to it and to living there. Take a few small items there each time you go. A few clothes. Some pots and pans. Take walks in the neighborhood. Move psychologically first.

See a lawyer. Move your portion of funds into a new, separate bank account in another bank. If he finds out from the statement and asks you about it, just tell him you needed the money you withdrew for some reason.

Since you do not want to live with him, find ways to keep yourself unavailable to him. Sleep in the same bed with him, if you want, but each time he wants to make love, refuse him. Don't worry about this driving him to the arms of the other woman, because you are leaving anyway.

If you do not want to sleep in the same bed with him, invent a project you are working on and make the spare bedroom your work and sleep place until you "finish" your project.

Most important of all, meet new men as set forth in chapters 9, 10, and 11. Force yourself. And do not tell them about your situation. Have dates with new men and have them pick you up at your secret apartment.

After two months, ask yourself how you feel about him. You should definitely feel stronger about yourself. You did not let his cheating undermine you or your strength of self.

Do you still want to leave? If not, stay as long as you want to. If you do want to leave, schedule the movers to come when he is gone.

If You Are Ready . . . Go. Clean everything out that is yours and leave. No note. Let him arrive home to find open and empty closets, open and empty drawers, and no explanation, no telephone number, no address. Lower the temperature several degrees, so that he literally feels the chill of your absence.

He may never contact you. If he does, do not give an explanation. If he wants to know why, tell him you don't know. You just do not feel the same about him and want a new life without him.

Or you can leave him a note saying you are seeing someone else— which you should be doing—and that you have moved in with him (if you have).

If you do not live with a man you considered monogamous to you and who cheated, do not tell him you know he has been seeing someone. Just get busy seeing other men. Cancel dates with him at the last minute and go out with someone else. Do not try to fake this by pretending there is someone else. *Get* someone else to go out with.

Be the Winner. You emerge the winner who outfoxed him if you make changes and do not ever let him know that it had anything to do with what he did. Let him think simply that he lost you. Atta girl!

If He Tells You He Has Been Unfaithful.
He may be trying to hurt you, or he may be trying to break up with you. If you can, simply listen without expressing any emotion.

When he finishes telling you, begin talking about something else, as if he had just told you some football scores and now you are turning the conversation to something that interests you.

If he brings the conversation back to his confession of infidelity, stay calm and ask, "Why are you telling me?" Put it back on him.

If he says he wants to see someone else, say, "I think that is an excellent idea.'' If he says he is telling you because he feels guilty and just wants to be honest with you, ask him, ''What do you want me to do about it?''

If he says he wants you to forgive him, say, ''Well, if I happen to confess to you that I have been unfaithful, too, would you be able to forgive, really forgive, me and never try to get even or to question me about it?''

He may then ask, ''Have you?''

Keep putting it back on him. Say, ''You have not answered my question.'' He is now the one on the defensive.

He may say, ''Yes, I would forgive you.''

''And never be punitive or question me about it?''

If he says, ''Yes, I agree not to,'' say, ''Good. Because I would never confess to something like that, so it is a waste of time for you to ask.'' Change the subject again, find a reason to leave or to have him leave. Be as sanguine as possible. Never bring it up again. But start finding other men to replace him right away.

Foil Him. He will have failed in his attempt to shock you, to see his power reduce you to nothing. Once he is gone, you can cry or rage, if you like, but you are the captain of your soul instead of him.

Let it be a lesson to you never to be committed to a man until you are married to him. He may still cheat if you are married, but you are in a stronger legal position then.

If you have been committed while single, you are now stranded with no one to fall back on. Starting over with a broken heart is the hardest thing in the world to do. But you must.

If He Leaves You. If he leaves you for another woman, *you did not fail.* And neither did he. The relationship had simply run its course, even though you may not feel it had run its course with you.

You may feel you want only him. That is a hurt ego talking—and it is natural for the moment. The truth is, you may think you know that you want him, but what you really want is fulfillment in love—and that is just not possible with him, so, obviously, then, he is not what you want.

Keep tuned in to the feelings of wanting fulfillment in love instead of wanting a particular man and you will have it. You will begin re-directing your behavior toward that end.

If He Comes Back to You. What if he comes back to you? This can become a back-and-forth game that can go on for years. You and he are having a hard time disconnecting. Going back and forth is a way of weaning yourselves from each other. Normally, it never works out. That is because a relationship has a hard time stabilizing once you become addicted to the emotional roller coaster of game-playing.

Two key ingredients are out of whack, which is why the relationship cannot settle into marriage. There is not enough peace and there is too much of a competitive struggle.

No Peace. Real love has the quality of peace. Peace is not boredom. Peace is fulfillment. Peace is the satisfaction that has no need to seek anything else. Peace is a self-contained joy within the relationship. It is whole.

Competitive Struggle. When two egos are on the line in a relation-ship, it is a no-win deal. There is one-upsmanship in the game-playing. There are petty victories, petty wounds. Jealousy becomes a dominant energy and resentment is close behind.

However, if it takes going back and forth for a long time before you finally get weaned from him or tire of the lack of fulfillment, then go ahead. Do whatever you must.

Whether you rave or go through game-playing, or however you han-dle it, promise yourself no regrets, no shame, no guilt, no scolding yourself for it later. Whatever you do, it is okay. You have the right to feel whatever you feel.

21

When Relationships End

A few seasons ago, I pulled on one of my favorite outfits, only to realize it was too out of fashion for me to wear anymore. It was a very glamorous outfit that I had worn on several occasions.

I wanted so much to wear it still. Turning it on the hanger, I thought of the wonderful times I had enjoyed in it. I held it to me and wondered if I could ever find another outfit with that same beautiful color. Sadly, it was not suitable for wearing anymore.

There are some relationships you outgrow in the same way. And there are those relationships that just cannot develop into what you need. They were wonderful a few years back, but they just don't work today. Most relationships were right for you at the time, just as last season's dress was. Your relationships didn't fail. The times simply changed both of you.

Oh, it is much, much harder to discard a relationship that you want so much to fit than it is a dress. Too much has gone into making it. Yet, like your favorite dress, there comes a time when a relationship has been altered as much as it can be and it still just won't work anymore.

Not all relationships last. That is the risk of love.

IF YOU ARE OUTGROWING THE RELATIONSHIP

If you are the one who is changing, try to preserve a man's ego as you move out of the relationship. There will be only so much you can do, but try to be kind. Tell him it has nothing to do with him. Thank him for all the wonderful times. This is a man who cares about you. That, in itself, says a lot of good about him.

IF HE IS OUTGROWING THE RELATIONSHIP

If you feel a man you care about changing toward you, and if you have a sexual relationship with him, ask him, *once*, to clarify his view of your relationship. Listen closely. Do not volunteer anything.

If he is vague or infers that he likes you as a friend, smile happily and say, "Good. That is what I was hoping to hear," even if it crushes you.

End It with Class

Have the class to walk away and not look back. Forget immature tactics to rekindle his love. No writing letters or sending cards. No thoughtful messages on his voice mail. No telephone calls for advice. No sending sentimental gifts that remind him of you. No indulging in fantasy that one day he will want you back.

Change the Relationship

Accept the fact that the relationship is ending. Don't destroy what you have had by trying to hang on or making a pest of yourself. Change the relationship, don't end it.

Make him your friend. Say to him, "Jonathan, it means a lot to me to have a friend like you. I have a wonderful girl friend I know you would like."

Launch into a description of her finer qualities and close by saying, "Of course, I hope, someday, you will return the favor if you know a man I might enjoy dating, too."

Don't have sex with him anymore.

You may find yourself feeling attracted again from time to time, but dismiss it and operate as a friend. If it is ever to be more, he must clearly state it to you. You will not be led on by occasional dates and flirtation.

Risk Vulnerability

If you try to move on, but find yourself stuck with regret, or worry that you could have done something different, go ahead and risk your ego and pride once and for all. It is far better that you completely reveal yourself and see that there was nothing else you could have done than to suffer anguish that prevents you from moving ahead. Sometimes, you just need to know you have done everything possible. In that case, go to him, tell him how much you love him, how you feel about losing him. If you break down and cry, do so with no sense of shame or regret. These are your emotions and you will not be ashamed of them.

If he still turns away—or if he tries again and it does not work—you will know you have done all that you could possibly have done. Knowing that should help you heal faster.

GETTING OVER HIM

There are three ways to expedite getting over him.

1. Call on a trusted friend.
2. Be a tough little street kid.
3. Shrink your problems.

Call on a Trusted Friend

There is a gentle, caring friend who knows how to comfort you if you call on her. Call that person over to your apartment. Ask your friend if she can simply listen without saying a word to you or to anyone else. Choose the three most painful moments in your relationship when you realized it was ending. Begin with the first event. Tell it in sequence, from beginning to end. See it happening again. Feel each moment. Describe the feeling. Cry if you want to. Feel every feeling.

Conclude it. Your friend should be someone who will not say a word, who will not judge or qualify and will sit quietly while you recount it over and over and over.

You have expended a lot of emotion and you are probably tired. When your friend leaves, eat something if you want to, take a bath, and go to bed.

Do this as often as possible. Your best friends will understand your need to do this. Like letting air out of a tire, you will have released a great deal of the sorrow in this way.

Relationships exist in our emotions. Therefore, we are entitled to feel whatever we feel. Allow yourself to feel everything. The emotion weakens each time you vent it, until it has no destructive control over you.

You may have a great deal of anger. Give yourself three choices of ways to handle your anger that will not hurt you or anyone else. Possible choices are:

- To beat, shred, or smash objects of no value until you are exhausted. Be sure you do not hurt yourself, ever!

- To write letters that are filled with all the anger you have—but do not keep them and do not mail them.

- To get into an exercise program that lets you work off the steam while you actively think of your anger.

Be a Tough Little Street Kid

There will come a time when you will either nurse yourself into a "victim mentality" or you will call on your tough little street kid, who is part of your inner self, too. This is your "survivor" instinct.

The tough little street kid inside you will send the inner nurse away. It will say, "Well, that was tough. But, hey, it happens to everybody. It's nothing special that it happened to me. Just one of the breaks in life. Time to get on." Your inner street kid takes heartbreak in stride and moves on.

Being a victim is a state of mind. Fortunately, you can change your state of mind. Changing yourself from victim to victor is a mental process. Victims do not experience fulfillment. Victims lose the people they love every time because that is all they know how to do. They have become lifetime buddies with their inner nurses.

Victims have nothing but the story of their victimization to make them feel special.

Claudia wept as she told me her story. When she met Grant, he had just broken off an engagement with a woman. Claudia and Grant soon decided to marry, too. Then, one day, she went to his apartment and found his former fiancée there.

A confrontation ensued and Claudia left in tears. Several months later, he reassured her that the relationship with the other woman was really over and Claudia took him back. They had just selected their wedding invitations when Claudia returned from a business trip to find his former fiancée in his arms again—in Claudia's home!

"Can you imagine how I felt?" she asked. "Can you? I was treated that way twice. Not once. Twice! *Me*. He was so bad to me."

Knowing it had happened eight years ago and that this pretty lady had dated dozens of men with unhappy results since then, I took a bold step.

"I can imagine it because it's nothing special, Claudia," I said. "It is just a typical part of developing romantically. It's no big deal."

Of course, it had been a big deal when it happened. But it had also been eight years and she had not forgiven herself for it. She continued to punish herself by living and reliving the victim role.

The ordeal had become too "special" to her. It was time to give her a true perspective.

I now have a wedding picture of Claudia that has a thank-you written on the back of it.

After she married her new man, she told me she appreciated my forcing her to get out of her self-pity, to stop playing victim, and to get on with being a winner at love. She could have married many years earlier *if she had not continued to nurse her victim role as special.*

Shrink Your Problems

Do not hesitate to work through your grief with a counselor. Get any and all help you need. A good psychologist will be able to help you see that no matter how awful the pain may be, no matter how sad you feel, that you, my dear, are still quite wonderful and deserve love.

* * *

Love is not just something you feel; it is also something you learn. It's no different from learning how to ride a bicycle, really. You take your falls, scrapes, bruises, and cry about it. But, one day, you learn how to balance on your bike and you are flying down the street like everybody else.

That's exactly how love is. Don't take it as a personal failure when you feel the pain of loss. It isn't. It just means you are working your way through it, learning how to experience love like the rest of us! Get back on—you'll make it!

22

Living Together — the Good, the Bad, and the Ugly

There are women walking down the streets of New York City who think they are carrying Gucci handbags, when, in fact, they may have bought pirated look-alikes. How can a woman know if she has bought a Gucci bag? If she buys it at a Gucci-authorized store.

How will you know if a man is genuinely committed to you in a relationship? If he marries you.

Why am I talking this way in a live-in society where singles talk about their committed relationships? *Single* and *committed* are contradictions in terms. If you want to get married, you must be very clear about understanding this, because hip talk can make you think you are getting the exact same thing when you aren't. Just like a pirated Gucci bag.

IT'S ONLY A PIECE OF PAPER

I think there are many justifiable reasons for a man and a woman to live together without marriage, but because of the stories I have heard from many clients, I want you to be aware of all sides of that arrangement. For instance:

Palimony became part of relationship vocabulary through a landmark case. A famous movie actor named Lee Marvin had lived with a beautiful young woman, Michelle, for years.

Marriage wasn't necessary for them (it was just a piece of paper, they claimed). She even had her last name legally changed to Marvin, like his, so they would seem married and sound married (after all, it was a committed relationship).

Apparently, Lee had been living with Michelle for six years when he took a business trip without Michelle, who remained at their residence in California.

However, Lee happened to run into his old high school sweetheart and stayed on a few days to spend time with her. Lee realized he was in love with her, and he married her (committed to her with a piece of paper) then and there.

You can call him a cad all you want to, it doesn't change the fact that *he knew the difference between living together and being married.*

Michelle found out about all this after his marriage. She received a financial settlement, but it wasn't what she probably would have gotten if she had been married to him—plus, she realized *she had never really had him. It had been make-believe.*

I tell this story because it is not uncommon. I have many sharp, well-educated women clients who have lived with men for years only to come home one day and find that they have moved out to marry other women.

When a man says "It's only a piece of paper," remind him that *the Constitution of the United States is only a piece of paper.*

DIVORCE STUDIES

Two separate articles in *USA Today* (November 29, 1994, and October 7, 1993) talk about a twenty-five-year study that shows a higher divorce rate among couples who lived together before marriage than among couples who did not live together before marriage.

Living together and marriage are much like identical twin babies, who look alike, however, they are two separate entities, despite their striking similarities.

Marriage and living together have different bases. The premise of marriage is "This will work." The premise for living together is "*let's see if* this works." Couples form their habits of how they relate to each other based on the premise of the relationship. Apparently, when couples have formed habits as live-ins for a number of years and then marry, they have difficulty making the transition into habits on a new premise.

Couples who have lived together for several years may finally marry out of obligation or as a quick fix for a relationship in trouble—or for both reasons, which will not work. This, too, would contribute to a higher divorce rate.

If you live with a man for a short period of time, it will not have a negative effect on your marriage. One month, six months, even eighteen months can be okay. But patterns begin to form around that time, so you want to seal the deal before then, if marriage is your goal.

I am not opposed to living together. I lived with my husband for three months before we married. If you have been living with a man for a number of years, do not worry about this. Statistics are guidelines, not rules. Say to yourself, right now, "I am not a statistic." Use the information to motivate yourself to get married to him or to someone else, if that is what you want.

WHEN YOU SHOULD LIVE WITH A MAN

Getting Your Life off Hold

Clarissa dated a man she loved for thirteen years. She slept with him but would not let him stay over, nor would she stay over with him. Several times during the thirteen years, he said, "Come on, Clarissa, let's move in together for six months and see if we want to get married."

Her answer was always the same. "No. Living together means you are not sure. I only want what is sure."

Living together does mean you are not sure, but it also means you desire a closer relationship. And love is a risk!

Six months is not that big a risk. It is a reasonable time in which to decide if a relationship will work out. Instead of holding out for thirteen years, Clarissa could have moved in for six months. Within six months she would have known, and so would he. If he claimed not to know, she would have her answer and could get on with her life. Thirteen years is too long to wait for a man to be sure he wants to marry you.

Don't Live Alone

I also think it can be better to live with someone you love and risk losing him, if he won't marry you, than it is never to have lived with a man. Women who have lived with a man—with or without marriage—know how to relate to men.

They understand living with someone. They are more flexible, soft, sensual, and have an inner instinct about men. They have a "humanness" about frailties and shortcomings in people. Women who have lived with a man, with or without marriage, can cultivate relationships with men easier than women who have never lived with a man.

THE MOST IMPORTANT QUESTION

If you want to marry at some point, the most important question you will want answered before you live with a man is "Has he ever lived with a woman before and later married her?" If so, how long? Did they marry? Did he marry a woman he did not live with? If he has been married more than once, did he live with one he did marry and with one he did not marry?

His answers are vital as to whether or not you live with him first—if your goal is to marry him. If he has lived with a woman and later married her, chances are he will do so again. People are repeaters. We all tend to repeat behaviors. However, don't live with him before marriage as long as she did, or your marriage may follow the same divorce pattern, too.

If, on the other hand, he has lived with women and never married them, back off! This man is not someone you should move in with, certainly not if you expect to marry him. There is always an outside chance of it happening, but it is not likely.

If he is a man who lived with his first wife before he married her, but has since lived with women without marriage, it can go either way.

You can always tell a man, up front, that you don't mind living together a month or two first, but that at that point, it makes sense for the two of you to get married. Get your blood tests and your marriage license before you move in together.

If he agrees to your terms, you should only talk and behave as if you are getting married. Three weeks into the situation, when everything is especially mushy and close, during a spontaneous moment of fun and excitement, have the name and address of a minister in your purse, along with your marriage license, for a sudden, romantic "I do"!

CAN YOU LIVE TOGETHER TO WORK OUT PROBLEMS BEFORE MARRIAGE?

What about working out problems in the relationship before you get married? Are you kidding me? Why on earth should anyone do that with a man she is not married to? That is what marriage is a commitment to do.

Listen to the marriage vows. Do they say, "I, Suzy, now that you, Jake, have gotten your act together and worked out all your problems in our relationship, do here take thee as my problem-free husband because the rest is easy"?

Hardly! It is "I, Suzy, now take you, Jake, for better *or for worse*, in sickness and in health, for richer or for poorer [in other words, whatever the problems may be], till death us do part." Now, that's a commitment to work out problems!

Don't believe anyone who says that you can work out problems before you get married. Marriage contains its own set of problems that cannot be worked out beforehand. That is because marriage operates under a completely different set of rules.

My final feeling about marriage as opposed to living together is this: If you are going to have all the headaches of a marriage, if you are going to have to put up with all the adjustments and problems of marriage, and if the relationship stands as much chance of ending in heart-break as marriage, you may as well be married.

After all, when it is over it hurts just as much as divorce, but at least you have the comfort of knowing it was a relationship you both cared enough about at one time to give your best shot!

How to Get Married

23

Love

⌒⌒

Love is not an emotion. Love is a power.
—GINIE SAYLES

A group of doctors at Brooke General Army Hospital in San Antonio, Texas, woke me up at five o'clock in the morning. They needed my permission, they said, to change my medication. If they did not change the medication, I would die. If the new medication did not work, I would die.

I was twenty-six years old and married to an army physician. The use of an intrauterine device (IUD) for birth control had landed me in intensive care, connected to machines and barely holding on to life.

I gave permission for the medication change. A month later, I was released from the hospital. Three months later, I woke at the same time the doctors had awakened me and then I had a dream.

I dreamed I looked out a window from the upstairs waiting room of a movie theater. I saw a three-tiered rainbow appear that began to glow. As it grew brighter, I became happier, then joyous, until I felt the brilliant light from the rainbow pull me through the window and into itself. I knew the radiant joy I felt could not intensify one more degree if I remained alive in my body. I wanted to stay in the rainbow's light, but I did not want to leave my four-year-old daughter. I saw the letters N-O pass out of my forehead and into the brilliant light that held me.

Like a tide sweeping out to sea, the rainbow, the light, the great joy, all swept from me. I awoke, sitting up, and burst into tears.

I cried for days, not knowing how to explain what I had experienced, knowing only that it was related in some way to my recent illness.

It was not until someone suggested it might have been a warning dream that I realized what it was. It was not a warning. There was no condemnation in it. For a reason I do not know, I was simply loved. It was a love that completely humbled me because of its magnitude in comparison with all my limitations.

It taught me what love is. Love is not an emotion. Love is a power. I believe now that we are all made of this beautiful substance of love and that when we see a person's value beyond his or her limitations, we experience love.

ACCEPTING HIS LIMITATIONS IS LOVE

One day you will realize that he is never going to be on time. One day you will realize he is never going to sail in the America's Cup, as he swears he will. One day you will realize he gets just as frightened as you do when there are strange noises outside. And one day you will know you will always have to remind him of the light at the intersection on Fourth Street.

That is the day you will realize that your man has improved within the framework of the relationship as much as he can. It is not that he does not love you; but to change further would be impossible. Besides, then you would have a different man altogether, and not him anymore.

A Man Has the Right to Be Who He Is

If you are trying to change him into someone else, you need someone else or you need to examine your expectations realistically.

Recently, on Lifetime, I saw a rerun of Barbara Walters's interview with the actor Walter Mathau. His wife said that his gambling is something that she refuses to let destroy all the good they have together.

She simply won't think of it. In other words, she sees his value beyond his limitations. She loves him.

Serious issues have to do with how a man treats you. And that is all you have the right to demand. Accept him, shortcomings and all, and you can experience love.

HOW YOU WILL KNOW HE LOVES YOU

And you will know he loves you because he will see the wonder of you and accept your limitations, too. You will know it, because:

- **Your relationship will be his priority**. One of my clients was upset that the man she was in love with was planning to attend a social to which she had not been invited. She left a message on his voice mail expressing her concern. He canceled the social and took her to dinner. He chose her feelings over an important invitation.

- **Being with you every day is automatic**. When he loves you, he wants to be with you. He meets you for lunch when you both can. He picks you up after work. He takes you with him to his tennis match. You go to the mall together. You shop for groceries together. He is not just a weekend lover.

- **He makes plans with you**. If he is talking about backpacking through Europe next year, it is not a good sign. But if he talks about the two of you backpacking through Europe together it is.

- **You become a part of his world**. You are included in his office party. When you meet his co-workers, they may have already heard of you. He discusses his career with you. He includes you in his interests.

- **He looks at you a lot when you are together**. You can tell if the steam has gone out of a relationship by watching couples. Steam is low if a man is sitting with a woman but turns sideways and looks around at everybody else or leaves her for long periods sitting by herself while he talks to buddies.

    A man in love sits with you. He faces you most of the time. He listens to you and talks to you. He touches you a lot. Most

telling of all, though, is that he looks at you more than at anyone
else.

- **He marries you**. The idea of marriage may take a little persua-
  sion or it may not, but he does it. He simply wants to live his
  life with you. He marries you.

24

Nine Reasons
Women Do Not Marry

1. THEY CAN'T FIND THE RIGHT MAN

When you can't find the right man, it is because there is a part of yourself you have not accepted. When you can't accept your imperfections, you can't accept imperfections in men. One of the exercises I have for clients who always feel they can't find the right man is that I have them "marry" themselves.

Haven't you seen women who do not look as good as you or take as good care of themselves as you, who don't accomplish as much as you, who make you wonder how on earth they married such great guys? Sure you have. The secret is, they married themselves a long time before they married men. Oh, such a woman may not have had an actual ceremony of marriage with herself, but she married herself all the same by accepting herself, flaws and all. You must marry yourself if you want to find the right man to marry you. It is that simple and that complex.

2. THEY WANT MEN WHO DO NOT WANT THEM

A woman who is really ready for marriage has no ego attachment to unavailable men. By that I mean that she is not challenged by men who are emotionally unable to commit. She does not yearn for a man who is in circumstances that make him unavailable—such as his being married or living with someone or being too busy to be with her or making her the last priority on his to-do list. Or a man who ''needs more time.'' More time for *what*?

3. THEY ARE STUCK IN A DEAD PAST

Sadness, bitterness, anger, and fear are all telltale symptoms of not living in the now but in the unchangeable past. There is fear of getting into another relationship that could hurt if it did not work out. The healthy use of fear is that it teaches you good sense in relationships. The unhealthy use of fear is to stop having relationships.

4. THEY ARE STUCK IN AN IMAGINED FUTURE

The woman who is stuck in an imagined future is easy to identify because she knows exactly what she wants in a man and exactly what she does not want in a man. She can tell you what he will be like and what their life will be like. She has a criteria list half a page long or longer. *But she is alone.*

Open yourself up today, to right now. The greatest relationship in the world that might be waiting for you in the future is not as important as the man who holds you in his arms right now.

The imagined future is a mental seduction that masks fear. It is so much easier to imagine what it will be like ''someday'' than to deal with relationships today.

A woman who is stuck in the imagined future is often a woman who believes in the myth of ''the one.'' This has done more to send women into old age without ever having taken the risk of love than any other myth.

So much of this is caused by the inability of a woman to adapt to human failings, human nature. The now is all you have for love.

5. THEY WANT TO GET MARRIED BUT DO NOT WANT TO DATE

A woman sat down for a consultation with me, let out a deep breath, and said, "I want to get married. I am even willing to pay to meet somebody. I just don't want to go through the process of looking for a husband again. I don't want to go to the trouble of having to get ready and go out. I dread the whole business of dating."

When you are ready for marriage, you will not dread the process of finding a mate. You will feel excited and energized by the process. You will have fun meeting lots of new men and living through all the new experiences you will have with different men.

What would you think if you heard someone say, "I want to be rich, but I don't want to have to earn it." You would know the person is not likely to get rich. Most people who make a fortune enjoy the whole process of making it as well as having it. It's the same way with dating and marriage. When you are really ready for marriage you will find enjoyment in the dating process itself.

6. THEY DON'T ACCEPT RESPONSIBILITY FOR HAVING RELATIONSHIPS

You are just as responsible for providing love and relationships for yourself as you are for providing physical shelter for yourself.

Begin to change your relationship life by saying, out loud, "I accept responsibility for all my relationships—past, present, and future." You will feel a new power enter your relationship life. Say it over and over and often!

"But, Ginie," you say, "I had some rotten relationships. I'm not going to accept responsibility for those!"

You are not responsible for how someone else behaves, but you are responsible for allowing the behavior to continue and for being in the relationship. At some point, each of us decides whether or not to allow someone to relate with us. And at all times, we are responsible for staying in a relationship with someone.

7. THEY ARE TOO UNSELFISH

You must want marriage for yourself, otherwise a man may lead you on for years until he decides to leave. And you must know how to stick up for yourself in relationships, to insist on being treated fairly, to refuse to be treated poorly. That is what marriage material is in a woman.

8. THEY ARE HIGHLY INVOLVED WITH FAMILY

Anytime a woman feels greater allegiance to her family than she does to her relationship with a man, she does not deserve to get married. If she were married, he would suffer unfairly in their marriage. A woman needs to make her choice of not involving her family in her love life and never confiding troubles she may be having with them.

9. THEY ARE WAITING FOR SOMETHING OR FOR SOMEONE TO CHANGE

In the past you might have thought you would be ready for someone to marry you "if" or "when" certain things happened in your life. Some of the excuses people use not to marry are: "Mother still needs me to look after her," or "Sam loves me but needs more time." Again, more time for *what*?

When people are really ready to get married, they get married and they don't fool around about it. When you are really ready to get married, and if you are dating someone who isn't ready to get married "yet," you may grieve inside, but you face facts that you are ready for marriage and you find a man who is also ready for marriage—and you marry each other.

Frequently, these are very happy marriages. They are marriages of "like mind" on the matter, and they are not trying to fool anybody.

As long as you have a reason not to marry—or as long as you tolerate a relationship with a man who has a reason not to marry—then, no matter what you say, you are not really ready to get married.

By buying this book you have shown that you are not just wanting and hoping to get married anymore. You are at least to the point of facing the truth and stopping yourself from making any more excuses.

25

Becoming Marriageable

A woman's marriageability runs like this, beginning with the most marriageable:

- A woman who has been married before and who has had children.

- A woman who has been married before and who has not had children.

- A woman who has never married but who has lived with a man and has had a child.

- A woman who has never married but who has lived with a man and has never had a child.

- A woman who has never married, has never lived with a man, and has never had a child.

As you can see, the key is the degree to which you have been interacting with men. The more you fulfill your biological destiny as a woman, the more marriageable you become. What I like about this is that you have control over your life. You can change it.

Interestingly, age is not the key factor, but women worry about it most. I find that women between the ages of thirty-eight and forty-six who have lived with a man or who are actively dating are very marriageable. This age period is when they come into their own as women and bloom. The level of interaction with men makes a woman more marriageable than her age.

Simply put, the more you have done something, the more likely you are to do it again and the easier it is to do it again. People tend to repeat patterns.

Marriage is its own attractant. People who have married before can marry again. There is a behavioral knowing, an easy style of relating that married people have. Women who have been married step easily into a married style of relating with men.

THE LANGUAGE OF MARRIAGE

Women and men who are divorced can marry more easily during the first two years after a divorce (unless it was unusually bitter) than they can later on. In fact, for every year past the third year after a divorce, the ability to remarry may slightly decrease.

Why? Because when women or men are newly divorced, they know how to be married. They are used to married life on many different levels of their psyches. They are more comfortable married than not married because they have lived within the framework of marriage for quite some time.

There is a married way of relating to the opposite sex that is easy, natural, and comfortable; an unembarrassed acceptance of unromantic chores, moods, body functions, and small vanities; a perspective of sex that is not magnified in meaning the way it often is in single people.

Sex is accepted in its lovely simplicity within an overall marriage relationship. That is why newly divorced people are initially uncomfortable with dating. They are more comfortable being married, and so they often move easily into marriage again very quickly. That is because during the adjustment period after divorce they are, psychologically, more married than single.

After a few years, they become more single than married. They slowly become more used to single life—and become fluent in the language of being single. They get used to being alone, to doing things alone, to not reporting to anyone, and to not taking anyone else into consideration when they when they want to do something.

They become more aware of flaws in other people. They begin to romanticize the idea of marriage and create an ideal marriage mate. They get a little pickier and less tolerant when someone doesn't fit this idealized mate. They become more self-conscious of mistakes they make with someone they are interested in, embarrassed about human body functions, and magnify sex beyond its meaning into either a sign of commitment, a battle of withholding and teasing, or, worse, a casual "score." All of this inhibits remarriage somewhat.

There is always a period of adjustment in any new marriage, but the conflict between expectations and realities is harder and more difficult between two people who have been divorced a long time or single a long time because they have to learn—or relearn—the language of marriage. Whereas, two people who meet and marry shortly after their divorces do not have to learn the language of marriage. They only have to adjust to each other.

WHAT IF YOU HAVE BEEN MARRIED SEVERAL TIMES?

Women sometimes tell me, "I am embarrassed to tell a man I have been married several times."

Naturally, we all want to have one shining lasting marriage, but life doesn't always work out that way in today's fast-paced, longer-life world. Most of the people you are going to be dating have been married once or twice before. That is life in today's single world. You should not be ashamed of having been married before.

Instead of hanging your head in shame and whispering that you have been married X number of times as a lowly confession, look at your life another way.

You have been loved before. A woman with a past is more interesting than a woman without one. If you have been married before—even badly—you have proven yourself to be a woman who is desirable enough to a man for him to marry you.

Never mind that you now regard your exes about as highly as you do subway terrorists; the fact remains that these are men who cared enough about you to marry you. Having been married numerous times may not be a badge of honor, but act as if it is! It is better than acting ashamed or cowed by it. It is proof positive that you are marriageable!

WHAT IF YOU HAVE NEVER BEEN MARRIED?

Women are just as embarrassed about having never been married. They complain that men ask them why they haven't married. Men ask if they have at least been engaged. These women want to know what to say.

Not ever having been married can mean whatever you want it to mean. I once read in "Dear Abby" that if someone asks you a question that is none of their business you are within your right to answer it any way you want to. I couldn't agree more.

Therefore, when you answer a man who asks, "Have you been married," you are equally within your rights to position yourself with as much strength as possible against his bias.

Society's Bias of Fear

The basic bias against an unmarried woman is that if a woman has not married before thirty-five she could be very hard to live with in marriage. Society feels this way because marriage is a daily series of trade-offs, of give and take, of negotiating what each one is going to do, of overlooking irritating habits.

When a woman is single she doesn't have to do any of that. If a woman has been single a long time, society's bias is that she may have rigid patterns that do not allow a man to be at home with himself, natural, at ease.

Understand the bias and then don't waste energy deploring it. Simply nullify it by saying whatever puts you to advantage as truthfully as you can so you and he can get past it and move into what really matters, which is enjoying each other in a relationship.

Vanna White, in her autobiography on audiotape, said that she went to California and tried to find an agent to represent her as a model. The agents would look at her approvingly, then ask, "How tall are you?" She truthfully said, "Five-six." Every time, the agents would say, "Oh, we only take models who are at least five-seven." Finally,

Vanna went to an agency and, when asked her height, said "Five-seven," and she was signed up as a model. The rest, of course, is history.

Did she lie or was she smart? I think she knew the truth was that she qualified in every way to be a great model. She knew that the industry bias against one inch was ridiculous. She was just as qualified whether she was one inch taller or not. Rather than resenting it, rather than arguing with it, rather than losing her chance, she brushed aside the cobweb of insignificance by interpreting the truth through her own reality of knowing she qualified as a model.

Do you qualify as a wife? Sure you do. So why let one word or one sentence slap a label on you that disqualifies you? I don't believe in lying, and I don't think Vanna White does, either; but I also don't believe in letting a stupid bias stop you from reaching your goals. Be on your side, like Vanna White. It can make a big difference in your life.

And don't be a crusader for a cause that won't keep you warm at night and comfort you. Get married and then crusade for a cause.

What can you say, then, if you are asked? You have to make up your own mind on the matter.

It's Up to You

Some women have said that they were briefly married before. These were women who had lived with a man and had felt married to him. They interpreted the truth through their reality. Plus, they knew that the laws of their state had a common law that would have considered their live-in relationships to be marriage.

Others have said that they lived with someone they thought they wanted to marry and changed their minds about. Still others have said they were once officially engaged.

One way to answer the question is to have a joyous, nondefensive attitude about the fact that you have not married. After all, if you have not married yet, it is not a personal failure. On some level, you were not ready before.

MAN: "Have you been married?"

YOU (smiling as if he had asked if you have ever gone sky-diving, answer brightly): "No, have you?"

MAN (answers yes, he has been married, then asks): "Why not?"

YOU: "Why not what?"

MAN: "Why haven't you been married?"

YOU (unruffled, smiling, and seeming amused by the question): "I didn't want to. Why did you get married?"

26

Do You Have a Marriage-Prone Relationship?

In my years of relationship consultation, I have found four mistakes women frequently make:

1. They do not have a marriage-prone relationship.

2. They stay single longer than they have to.

3. They miss marrying someone they could have married.

4. They "psychologically premarry" a man.

A MARRIAGE-PRONE RELATIONSHIP

A marriage-prone relationship has two striking features:
1. High-frequency dating
2. The same level of interest

HIGH-FREQUENCY DATING

One of the biggest clues to the seriousness of a relationship is the frequency of dating between a man and a woman.

A woman sometimes comes to me complaining that a relationship she has been in for quite some time has not moved into marriage.

I ask her how often she dates him. If she says "Once a week," I tell her that this is not marriage-prone dating.

If a man is dating you only once a week, you are casually dating. Out of thirty days in a month, he is seeing you four or five of them. He sees his postman more often than that!

He is spending more time without you than with you. What is he doing the other twenty-five or twenty-six days each month?

When a man gets serious about you, he wants to be *with* you—and often! The more serious he is, the more activities he wants you involved in with him.

Marriage is an everyday relationship, not a once-a-week dinner-and-sex date. (Although there are companionship dating scenarios like this, especially among much older single couples or married men who visit another town once a week. This works out fine because it is simply companionship and sex between two people who like each other but who do not have a serious enough level of interest in each other to prompt marriage.)

Yes, a relationship that starts out this way could end in marriage—but only if the level of interest changes from four or five days a month to a much higher frequency. This is how you will know a man is getting more serious.

What is an acceptable frequency of dating for the probability of marriage? A minimum of three days a week—and preferably more!

THE SAME LEVEL OF INTEREST

As with the bona fide relationship, you and the man you are dating must have the same or a similar level of interest in each other. If a man you are dating is much, much crazier about you than you are about him, you do not have a marriage-prone relationship, unless you simply decide to go ahead and marry him.

If you are much, much crazier about a man you are dating than he is about you, you do not have a marriage-prone relationship.

STAYING SINGLE LONGER THAN YOU HAVE TO

Many women stay single longer than they have to because of one word—*criteria*. Any time a woman says "I want a man who is a certain age range, height, weight, a certain education level, who has a sense of humor, who likes children and pets, enjoys outdoor activities, is a vegetarian, doesn't drink alcohol, etc." I know that this woman is not ready for marriage.

A criteria list is really a death list that kills any real relationship before it gets close enough to hurt. It is a list of reasons not to love someone. A criteria list is a shield of fear. When a person has been severely hurt before, it is understandable that he or she might feel a certain amount of fear for a brief period. But to talk about your criteria list is actually to advertise your fear. Your criteria list is the shield you hold up in front of yourself as if to say, "I am not going to get hurt again the way I did the last time. Next time, I'm going to get everything I want on this list!"

Psychology shows that when we make a list of what we want in a mate, we have really written down our own character traits that we hope also to find in a man.

When a woman is really ready for marriage, the first thing that changes is her criteria.

Three Ways to Set Criteria

There are three ways to set criteria for a marriage mate.

1. No criteria.
2. Soul-search criteria.
3. Three character traits.

No Criteria. The first and best way to set criteria is to have no criteria. Each man stands on his own merit, without comparison to any other man, without any list whatsoever. That means instead of looking for what might be wrong with him, you look at what is right with him.

No criteria also means that you look at the relationship mix between you and value it because it is different. **How does your relationship with him make you feel about yourself?**

Soul-Search Criteria. The second way to set criteria is to seek a soulmate. A soulmate has only one criterion—a feeling that fulfills your single greatest need in a relationship. A soulmate is connected to your soul through an emotional need that you long to have fulfilled. When that one special feeling is met, there will be many other needs that will also be satisfied.

Where should you look for your soulmate? In your soul. Tonight when you go to bed, close your eyes and ask yourself, if you were married right now, what is the one feeling you would want to have most of all? Just one. Concentrate on the feeling.

This one feeling gives your soul an emotional compass to guide you to the type of person who will provide this feeling for you in marriage.

If you have many different feelings, your emotional compass's needle cannot stabilize in a specific direction that moves you toward fulfillment. Don't scatter your shots. Concentrate on the one most important feeling.

You have more than one soulmate. If not, then what if your soulmate died when you were three years old? You are stuck, aren't you?

No need to worry. Your soul is made up of many different elements. Therefore, your soul can find nourishment and fulfillment from men whose souls also contain those elements and therefore connect to your soul.

You will know a man is one of your soulmates when he fulfills the one most dominant desire in your life that you wish for in a marriage. Your emotional compass will register in his direction.

Three Character Traits. The third way to set criteria is to choose three character traits that are necessary for you to be able to live with a man. Only three. This is the method I used, although I believe the no criteria method is best.

In my case, I wanted a man who was kind, because I could never allow myself to live with a man who was cruel. I also wanted a man who was generous-hearted. I do not like selfish men who cannot give of themselves. I wanted a man with a bountiful spirit, whose presence says, "Come, feast at my table."

So, in order to live with a man in marriage, I wanted a man who is kind and generous.

The third trait was sexual compatibility. You are going to be living with this man as his wife, which means he has conjugal rights to enjoy sex with you. It was important to me for my husband and I to be sexually compatible.

When you start listing more than three traits—two character traits plus a basic sexual compatibility trait—you go back into the defeating list.

In my case, I did not care about a man's age. He could be older than me, younger than me, or my age. I did not care about his height. I did not care about good looks. I did not care about his weight. I did not care about his level of education.

I cared that he would be kind, generous, and sexually compatible.

My husband is a very nice looking man who has a nice physique. He is older than me, taller than me, and very well educated.

I did not marry him for any of those reasons. I married him only because he is kind, generous, and sexually compatible.

When you begin to set criteria based on what you can live with, you will end up with so much more in a man than your list could ever give. Why limit yourself to a feeble list?

TIMING YOUR RELATIONSHIP FOR MARRIAGE

There are many women who could have married a man they wanted to marry if they had been aware of timing in the relationship. Timing is everything.

In my experiences as a stockbroker and as a relationship consultant, I have found that a relationship behaves very much like a hot stock. It has three phases. In phase one, it shoots up quickly, then plateaus as phase two, and either goes on up or goes down in phase three. Timing marriage, which is an emotional investment, is every bit like timing a stock for your financial investment.

Phase One

Once a couple's interest heats up to frequent dating, the relationship shoots up like a rocket with passion, intensity, excitement in being together, which is known as falling in love.

This period lasts an average of three to seven months, sometimes longer. It can be the easiest time frame in the course of a relationship for getting married. You are both in love and you know it. You want to please each other. And you want to be together.

Most people who marry know they want to marry each other very soon in their relationship. It clicks. It fits the way a dress either does or doesn't fit, and you know it. You don't have to figure out whether or not the dress fits. You know it as soon as you try it on.

I've known couples who dated for ten years, got married, and then divorced six months later. It does not take a long time, certainly not years. My husband and I married less than five months after we met, and we are now in our twelfth year of marriage.

After I explained marriage timing in a recent seminar in Houston, a woman approached and said, "Ginie, I just came out of a seven-year relationship. You are right about the timing of marriage. Earlier today, I told my best friend that there is just a small window of opportunity for marriage in the beginning of a relationship, and if you miss it, you can't get it back."

Phase Two

If marriage does not happen during Phase One, then at some point the relationship enters a second phase. It will begin to plateau, to level off and travel more in a straight line. On the average, the plateau period lasts from six to eighteen months, but I have seen a plateau period last as long as twenty-eight months.

The plateau is a good period. The madly-in-love stage is past, but your relationship is deepening, growing. This time is also a good time for getting married.

Phase Three

If marriage does not occur during the plateau period, the relationship will eventually enter a third phase of very, very gradual descent. At first, it is hardly noticeable. There may be some moments of magic occasionally, but those become fewer. Conflict increases until there is more unhappiness than overall happiness in the relationship. Eventually, the relationship degenerates to the point where it ends.

If marriage occurs during this third phase of a relationship, it is not going to work. At this point, couples marry as a Band-Aid for the relationship or out of obligation.

Band-Aid Marriages. A man may say to himself, "We are fighting so much now. Suzy has always wanted us to get married. Maybe if we marry that will make her happy. Maybe getting married will solve the problem and things will settle down and get back to normal."

Band-Aid marriages seem to improve relationships for a while, but the problems resurface because the relationship was allowed to deteriorate through lack of commitment. Marriage is a last-ditch effort to rescue the ailing relationship.

Obligation Marriages. A woman may say to herself, "I don't really feel in love anymore, but Joe stood by me when my father died. All our friends consider us a couple. I would look like a cad if I didn't marry him now." A man may say, "I have lived with Cindy this long. I owe it to her to marry her."

Obligation marriages in phase three do not fare well. Obligation creates too heavy a toll eventually on the one who felt obligated, then resentment, then rebellion.

Getting married during a mutually happy period is the best time. No one is "giving in" because of problems or obligation. Therefore there is a greater willingness to work on problems as they arise, which then carries a marriage relationship to greater heights and deeper depths.

PSYCHOLOGICALLY PREMARRYING

What does it mean when a man tells you he loves you and wants to marry you at some point but that he is just not ready yet?

It means no.

What if he says he will marry you after he finishes a business deal he is working on, or when he gets back from Europe, or as soon as he finishes law school? Time goes by for you while dealing with his postponement.

Postponement means one thing—no.

The hardest part for me to tell you is that when he is stalling, it usually means that he hasn't found the woman he wants to marry yet. Even if it is just a case of his not being ready for marriage, you run the risk that when he is ready for marriage, he may want someone else entirely.

Herman came to me with a problem. He had been involved with Julie, a woman he cared about very much, for nine years. Julie had wanted to get married since the first year, but each year Herman felt he wasn't ready and had successfully kept Julie waiting.

Three months before he came to see me he met Madeline and fell head over heels in love with her. He wanted very much to marry her. He came to me because he wanted to resolve his conflict and learn how to break it off with Julie, who had been expecting him to marry her every year for nine years.

When a man is stalling you, it means you do not have the same goals for the relationship. It means you do not have a marriage-prone relationship with this man. Furthermore, it means that you need to be moving on down the line if you want to get married in this lifetime.

You may feel you do not want to marry anyone else but him. That is a tough situation, because it isn't going to happen as long as he can successfully put you off.

If you are not seeing other men, it means you are psychologically premarried to this man. Men need to earn your commitment through the contract of marriage. If you give your commitment away cheaply to their promises and delays, it may never occur.

When you refuse to play the commitment-but-not-marriage game and you decide to see other men, you will have one of the following outcomes:

- He will marry you.
- He will continue to see you, tantalizing you with false hope that he will come through, but he will still delay.
- He will stop seeing you.

He Will Marry You

You stand a greater chance of marrying the commitment tap dancer if you refuse to be suckered in to dating only him. Simply say, "I see no reason to stop dating other men until I am married. After all, that is what commitment really is. So, when I decide to marry, that is when I will commit to someone. Otherwise, what is the point?"

State it as if it is your decision, not his. And it is. It is your decision for your life. He is not making choices for your life that make you unhappy. You are, by staying with him. You cannot make him change, because you do not have control over him. You only have control over you.

At that point, he may say that the point of commitment without marriage is to see if the relationship can work before getting married. Sounds good, huh? Nope—it's another sucker's game that puts you out of circulation, where you might meet a man you could happily marry, and quickly. It is a game that denies you choices of other men. This makes you vulnerable to delay tactics and stalling, which puts you increasingly at a disadvantage.

And, of all things, if you agree to commitment without marriage and then if the relationship does not work out, you have to start all over, relearning how to meet men, feeling self-conscious, a bit older, behind in the marriage process, and you have lost precious time that could have been used in building a marriage.

So, say to him, "I think commitment without marriage is a coward's game. The purpose of dating is to eventually find someone you want to marry. We can continue dating, but until I decide to marry, I will not stop seeing other people."

He Will Continue to Date You and Tantalize You with False Hope

Unfortunately, your decision to keep other men in your life may not make your commitment tap dancer wake up to see what he is losing in you.

He may not change one bit. You will begin seeing other men, worrying the whole time you are with them about what he is doing. You may check your voice mail during your dates to see if he has called.

You may show up with a date in places where you know he hangs out. You may get drunk and cause a scene or leave messages on his voice mail or drive past his house after you get home from a date to see if he is out.

You may write an angry letter, venting your frustrations. Later, when he doesn't respond, you may write another letter that shows you really understand the situation, leaving the door open for him to call.

When he does not respond, you may write half a dozen more letters, each time thinking this letter is the one that will make him understand and fix the whole situation.

You may make up reasons to call him. It does not matter what your excuses are; he is always glad to hear from you. Unfortunately, he still gives you the story that he loves you and wants to marry you . . . but he just can't right now.

Same song. Second verse.

Nothing changes. Nothing gets resolved. Day and night, you feel panic at the thought that he will let you go. It is a real test of nerves.

He Will Let You Go

And if he lets you go, you will know clearly that he did not want to marry you. He may care for you, but if he had wanted to marry you, he could not have let you go.

It hurts, I know, but be proud of accepting responsibility for your life and moving courageously, if painfully, out into a future where there are men you can marry.

27

Bring Up Marriage Like a Winner

At some point, the subject of marriage has to be introduced. If he brings it up, fine. But, if he does not bring up the subject of marriage, then it is up to you.

Be aware of timing. So many women, waiting for a man to propose and having too much pride to propose themselves, get left behind by waiting until their best timing is past.

HAVE A TIME FRAME FOR GETTING MARRIED, NOT A DEADLINE

You will be more effective if you give yourself a time frame for your goal of being married than if you give yourself a deadline.

A time frame is basically the same thing as a deadline, except that it has flexibility, a period of time that makes you aware that you are operating within your final goal period.

Instead of saying, "My goal is to be married by June thirteenth," say instead, "My goal is to be married during the spring." Time frames allow you to enter your final goal period without being a failure. Take into account your personal goal and the reality of its being accomplished by then.

Once you know your inner time frame, here are some ways to bring up marriage like a winner:

Why Not Propose?

Glamorous movie star Zsa Zsa Gabor was on a talk show with me. She has been married eight times, and she said that she proposed to most of them. "Dah-ling," she said in her lovely accent, "a woman simply can't wait for a man to make up his mind what he wants to do when she knows what she wants to do."

Beautiful Georgette Mosbacher has been married three times, and she proposed to every one of them—and weren't they lucky?

If you love a man and you want to marry him, say something like this, "You love me, don't you?" Say it with sparkly enthusiasm that requires a yes. If he mumbles that he thinks so or doesn't know, don't back down.

Laugh and say, "Oh, yes, you do love me and you want to marry me, too!" Give him an excited kiss. "It's only two weeks until summer. Let's get married in Atlantic City [or Las Vegas, or wherever]. Just the two of us—and surprise everybody when we get back!"

Even if he refuses, you have proposed with strength. It is far better than a half-whining "Are we ever going to get married?" or an overly serious expression that looks as if you have drawn your sword and expect battle to begin. That is not speaking as if you expect him to agree.

If you simply cannot propose, the next suggestion may be for you.

Introduce A Competitor—A Man From Your Past

The Six-Month Cut-off: If a man has not brought up the subject of marriage by the sixth month of dating, then it is vitally important you introduce a competitor.

Who is the competitor? Well, the most convenient and effective one is a man from your past. Most women have had a man in their lives who liked them more than they liked him. In fact, if they think about it, they know that if they had encouraged him, he would have married them. In this scenario, we will refer to that man as Joe.

Early in your relationship with your new man, when he asks about your past, you tell him about Joe as a man you dated a couple of years ago who wanted to marry you but you just weren't ready for marriage at that time. You eventually had to break up with him because of it.

He may ask if you didn't marry Joe because you didn't love him. Say that Joe was definitely a man you could have loved if the time had been right, but that you just were not ready for marriage at that time.

Your new man may then ask if you think you are ready now. Smile and ask, "Is that a proposal?" If he says "Yes," then you can cinch the deal with a wedding date.

But if he says no, that he was just asking, say "I am more ready now than I was two years ago." Then change the subject. No more talk on this topic. Don't refer to Joe anymore.

A few months later, and if the subject of marriage has not come up, you have a tool for introducing the subject of marriage without seeming to.

You can say, "Oh, by the way, Joe called a couple of days ago."

"Joe?"

"Yes. Remember, I told you about him some time back? He was the man who wanted to marry me when I wasn't ready."

"Oh yeah, yeah . . . Joe. . . . What did he want?"

"He just called to see how I am. He asked if I am still the same . . . or if I have changed my old attitudes since we saw each other last."

"Oh? What did you tell him?"

"I told him about us."

"Really? What did he say?"

"He asked me what our intentions are. I said I didn't know what he meant. He said, 'Well, you know what my intentions have always been. What are this guy's intentions?' "

"What did you say?"

"I told him we haven't discussed it, but I said I would talk to you about it and get back to him and let him know."

Silence.

"So . . . let's talk about our intentions with each other . . . [silence] . . . so I can let Joe know. What are *your* intentions?"

"Well, I have always thought we would get married . . ."

"I thought so, [not acting surprised] and since we both feel that way, then . . . as Alec Baldwin said to Kim Basinger, 'Let's go ahead and get married and get on with our lives.' ''

Dream-Scenario

If you are really shy about it, there are people who have said the following, some of them with good results:

"I dreamed the other night that you asked me to marry you."

"Really? What did you say?"

"I don't know. I woke up. What do you think I should have said?"

The Challenge

If you think this man is a hard sell on marriage, and if you have never given your position before, say "It will take a special man to get me to the altar."

The Ultimatum

Ultimatums are hard to live up to when you are in love with someone. You flare up in anger, vow never to see him again if he won't marry you, and storm out in a huff of determination. Hours later, your raw nerves are running up and down through your body in wild electrical currents of fear.

You can't stand it. You want to see him. Maybe you handled it wrong. Maybe you'll never see him again. Maybe he'll find someone else. If you could just talk to him again and explain it better . . . If you write him a letter that puts it better than you did . . . if, if, if, maybe, maybe, maybe. You are consumed with self-doubt, anxiety, and the total need to see and be with this man.

Only, you just got through telling him you will never see him again if he doesn't marry you. And here you are a nervous wreck—and, worse, you are already trying to figure out a reason to justify seeing him again.

Some ultimatum. Ultimatums make a fool out of you, mincemeat of your pride, and can make a man gradually think less of you as he sees the total power he has over you.

Still, as bad as they are, sometimes they are all you have. And sometimes—if you can stick it out, raw nerves and all—sometimes an ultimatum works! But there is always the chance it won't.

Your best bet when giving an ultimatum is to say, "I love you and want to marry you. I believe you love me and want to marry me, too. You have said this is not the right time for you to marry. And I do not want any man to marry me if he does not want to.

"However, this is not the right time for me to wait anymore. If you want to marry me next month, and if you believe we can be happy together, leave a message with my voice mail during the next three days and let me know. Because after that, I am going on with my life." Leave. Do not call. Do not stay home. Do not be available until you hear his voice on your machine telling you that he wants to marry you.

AGREEING TO GET MARRIED

Make It the Number-One Priority for Both of You

Once you and your man decide to get married, agree that getting married will be the top priority for both of you, over anything else and anyone else. And that once you are married, your marriage will remain the number-one priority for both of you.

The beauty of marriage with this foundation is that it has a compass. You and your mate are not just shooting in the dark. You know the guideline and you measure everything of importance by that guideline.

The Secret to Success Is the Word *Secret*

Unless you have a great desire for a formal wedding with lots of guests, you may find you are better off just getting married without a lot of fanfare. Some women have found their grooms chickened out just from the pressure of a large wedding. But that is rare.

Get his input. If he really does not want a big wedding, compromise by having a private ceremony for just the two of you somewhere and then a lavish ceremony a month or two later.

Get Married

"Aaron and I are getting married as soon as he finishes computer school," Debbie said happily.

"Wonderful! When will he graduate?"

"He only has two and a half years left."

"Oh. Uh . . . well . . . congratulations, Deb."

Once the two of you decide to get married . . . *get married*. In our high-tech, fast-paced world of the twentieth century, long engagements are passé. Long engagements fit the pace of slow-moving time periods when people lived all their lives in one town or one region.

Sometimes long engagements work out, but more often they don't.

It is foolish to announce intentions to marry more than a year away. Anything can happen in a year. And it is doubly foolish if you have no engagement ring.

In order to keep your vow that your marriage to each other is the number-one priority to both of you over anyone and anything else, go ahead and get married. Your marriage can be your greatest resource. Why wait?

28

How You Can Be the Heroine of This Book

Your own love story waits only for its heroine—*you.*

You can be the heroine of this book if you implement those parts that apply to your life and implement them right now.

When you are single, the easiest thing to do is to passively think that all those great relationships will begin sometime soon, any day now, sometime this year, later on, just around the corner . . .

What really happens is that time goes by in short days and brief months until one day you realize years have passed in a state of suspended relationship life.

Use this book to pull your love story into the now. The now is the most valuable thing you have.

LOVE EXISTS ONLY IN THE NOW

For those of you with a spiritual bent, you can magnify your spiritual awareness a thousandfold in relationships by realizing that the most spiritual way you can live is in the now.

Have you seen women who are locked in a time warp? They still dress in the styles of the sixties or the seventies or the eighties. They mostly listen to golden oldies radio stations. You will know if you are not living in the now if you are wearing the same hairstyle and using the same makeup that you used three years ago. Change keeps you current and in the now.

Do you wake up each morning excited and joyous about a beautiful new day of opportunity? If so, you are living fully in the now, each day, by choosing that mental and emotional state.

You cannot feel happiness yesterday or tomorrow. You can only feel happiness, joy, excitement, and enthusiasm now, today.

One of the reasons we thrill to falling in love is because we so fully experience each moment with tingling life—and we feel it *now*.

And one of the greatest dangers to a relationship which threatens love is when couples stop relating to each other in the *Now*. You will know this has happened if the conversation becomes "itemizing" rather than "relating."

Couples itemize when they talk in lists. "Don't forget to pick up the cleaning and get the car washed." Some of this talk is necessary in day-to-day living; but when most talk is reduced to itemizing, the couple has shifted out of the emotional Now and into a substitute for relating.

Relating is sharing observations, laughter, experiences, details, comfort, encouragement, sadness, exercise, affection, and feelings in your talk and your behavior.

IS YOUR LIFE DESIRE-BASED?

There are those who seek to eliminate all human desire. But what is it that impels them so fervently to do this? Their very own desire for what they call inner peace. So, you see, there is no escaping it. Their desire to avoid desire means only that they have no faith in the fulfillment of their desire.

Desire is the basis of all progress. It is only as good or as bad as the channel you give it. Desire is the motivation of life. And you are the essence of all your desires.

Never be ashamed of desiring love, marriage, and family. These desires show that you are healthy.

If you follow your healthy desires, you will receive fulfillment. These are desires you are reaching for now, for fulfillment now. They are not daydreams for "someday." Daydreams for someday take the life out of you because they are always "someday." Daydreams are passive.

Desire is now. You want it now and it exhilarates you and moves you into action moment by moment.

Faith is not needed if you have no desire for something to be fulfilled. Faith occurs at the point when you desire something so much that you are willing to take the risk of failing in order to have it. Trust desire. When you desire something, it means that elements of it are already within your reach.

There are several layers of energy that operate like radio frequencies. Each level of energy contains elements that become yours when you enter that flow of energy.

The energy of love is positive. You can identify people who are in that energy frequency. They express anticipation and happiness that are elements of the love energy. You enter the energy field of love through desire, faith, and risk.

There comes a point in pursuing your desire when you know you are in a radiant peak of readiness because you really believe men are wonderful; you really believe you are wonderful; you really believe sex is wonderful. Desire has brought you to this heightened point—and it is at this point that you know this is all that can be done—and you do not stop, you simply let go.

You release *you* into the moment—just as a trapeze artist releases her grip from the bar and soars into a spin, reaching for the other bar. She experiences the same feeling that will accompany your moment of release.

You have entered the energy of love. Your love story has begun!

Send a self-addressed stamped envelope for a list of products by Ginie Sayles. Write to:

Ginie Sayles
Drawer 10007
Austin, Texas 78757

And remember:

Ginie gives seminars around the country. Write to her, requesting a schedule of when she will be in your area.

Your group or organization may host Ginie for a seminar on *The Seduction Mystique*. Send for more information today! Ginie also offers a limited number of private, one-on-one consultations with individuals.